Walks Through History
GLOUCESTERSHIRE

Walks Through History
GLOUCESTERSHIRE

JOHN WILKS

breedon **books**
PUBLISHING

First published in Great Britain in 2001 by
The Breedon Books Publishing Company Limited
Breedon House, 3 The Parker Centre, Derby, DE21 4SZ.

Other titles in this series:

**Walks Through History: Derbyshire ISBN 1 85983 166 4
Walks Through History: Kent ISBN 1 85983 118 4
Walks Through History: Oxfordshire ISBN 1 85983 229 6**

ISBN 1 85983 228 8

Printed and bound by Butler & Tanner Ltd, Frome, Somerset
Cover printing by GreenShires Ltd, Leicester

Contents

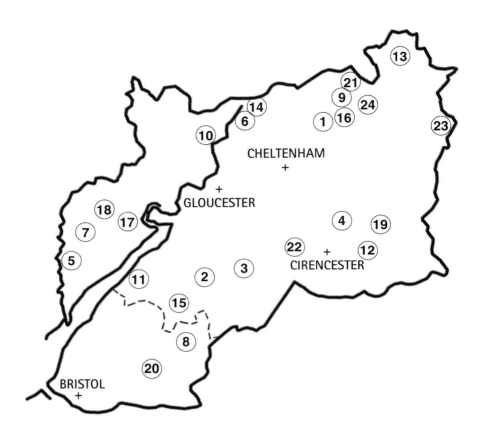

CHELTENHAM
+

+
GLOUCESTER

CIRENCESTER
+

BRISTOL
+

Walks through historic Gloucestershire
A brief historical introduction

Each walk in this book has been chosen not only because it is a pleasant walk in its own right, but also because it goes past sites which reveal the rich and varied history of the county. The walks are arranged chronologically, each walk having a major historical theme, and together they take the walker through 5,000 years of Gloucestershire's history. The purpose of this introduction is to show how each of the walks in this collection fits into the overall history of the county.

For much of its history, Gloucestershire was a frontier. It was the border of the Roman Empire, the limit of the advance of the pagan Saxons, the border between the Celtic and the Roman churches, the frontier of Norman England. For much of its history too, it has been a gateway to the western ocean. Man entered the county from the west from the Iron Age onwards, and trade with Europe and the Americas has flowed through its ports. In addition, Gloucestershire has been rich agricultural land throughout its history, and the story of wool is very much part of the story of the county. Included in the county in this book are parts of the former county of Avon. Until 1974, Bristol and its hinterland were part of Gloucestershire, and no history of the county could be complete without including these.

The first men who came to Britain were nomadic hunter-gatherers, who lived on roots and berries and those animals they could catch by hunting. They came into south-east England across a land bridge connecting Britain to mainland Europe, and gradually migrated inland, following the vast herds of wild deer and cattle. These primitive men entered the area known today as Gloucestershire around 400,000 years ago, slowly spreading along the high ground that flanked the Thames valley and eventually reaching the eastern slopes of the Cotswolds.

Early Stone Age man lived in the open air in temporary camps, leaving no mark upon the environment apart from occasional discarded tools found on the Cotswolds. It was not until around 4000 BC that man abandoned his nomadic existence, planting crops instead of gathering them from the wild, domesticating animals rather than hunting them, and building permanent homes. The first settlements avoided the wet and heavily forested plains of the Severn and Thames valleys, but were instead on the lighter soils of the Cotswolds valleys. These first domestic buildings, wooden and without foundations, left no mark upon the landscape. However, from 3000 BC onwards Stone Age man did build great communal burial mounds of stone called long barrows, mostly along the crest of the Cotswolds. These tombs, such as Belas Knap (walk 1) and Hetty Pegler's Tump (walk 2) survive until this day.

During the Stone Age the population of Britain was no more than 20,000 people, and within Gloucestershire man numbered a few hundred at most, living in family groups. But as the climate became warmer and agricultural techniques improved, the population grew rapidly. However, even during the Bronze Age (2000 BC onwards) Gloucestershire remained thinly populated compared to the Wessex Downs to the east. Trade increased dramatically in the Bronze Age, and the Bristol Channel and Severn estuary became a major trade route, connecting Ireland and Wales with the Thames valley. It was along this trade route that the first Iron Age settlers entered Gloucestershire from around 550 BC onwards. Iron was superior to bronze for making tools and weapons, and these new settlers, entering the region from the mouth of the Severn and up the Thames valley, gradually ousted the existing communities. As the population grew, families congregated into extended clans and tribes, each with their own territories. To defend the land they occupied, these tribes built strong hill forts as centres of power and trade. The Cotswolds ridge is lined with forts such as Uley Bury (walk 2). The iron deposits of the Forest of Dean were first exploited at this time, and iron ore was exported across all England and abroad.

Around 100 BC a tribe called the Dobunni entered Gloucestershire, arriving from Europe by sea up the Severn estuary. The Dobunni were very advanced, not only in weaponry but also in trade and social organisation, and easily assimilated or conquered the existing population. The Dobunni rapidly occupied all of modern Gloucestershire east of the Severn, as well as much of the surrounding counties, and established a flourishing and sophisticated capital at Minchin-hampton (walk 3).

The Dobunni kingdom split in two around 10 AD, one half becoming a client of the neighbouring Catuvellauni, the other remaining independent. When the Romans invaded in 43 AD, the independent Dobunni allied themselves with the invader, who built a base, Cirencester, on Dobunni land as a regional headquarters.

The Catuvellauni and their allies resisted, were rapidly defeated, and faded from history.

By 47 AD the Romans had subjugated the whole of southern England, and established a frontier from the Severn estuary to the Wash. A military road, the Fosse Way, ran along this frontier, serving the forts and garrisons established for its protection. Gloucestershire was a frontier zone, under military rule. Forts were built at Gloucester and Kingsholm, and a garrison town established at Cirencester. During the 70s, the invasion moved on, into Wales and the Midlands, and Gloucestershire was handed over to civilian control. Gloucester and Cirencester grew into proper towns, centres of trade and industry controlling the rich agricultural land of the Severn and the upper Thames valleys. The Forest of Dean, with its rich iron ore deposits, remained under military control, criss-crossed by roads and with iron foundries at Lydney and Cinderford.

Gloucestershire remained a frontier zone for the Romans for another hundred years, and Roman civilisation took longer to become established here than anywhere else in southern England. Farming remained based upon pre-Roman villages until the end of the second century, and few villas were built in Gloucestershire until after 200 AD. By then the aim was to incorporate the native population into the Roman Empire, giving them the benefits of Roman civilisation and thus giving them a stake in the defence of the Roman way of life. Cirencester became one of the four regional capitals of the Province of Britain, an important and sophisticated town, and rich villas such as Chedworth (walk 4) became centres of rural life.

By the end of the fourth century the Roman Empire was under threat from many directions, and Britain was increasingly harassed by pirates. In 410 AD, the Romans evacuated Britain, needing all available troops to protect Rome itself. Centralised government in Britain rapidly collapsed, and the island deteriorated into a series of mini-kingdoms and city states that had to defend themselves as best they could. Irish pirates came in increasing numbers up the Bristol Channel, initially for plunder but later to colonise. For several decades Gloucester and Cirencester resisted these advances before finally succumbing. Meanwhile Saxons, who were entering England in increasing numbers from Germany, were moving up the Thames, and overrunning Gloucestershire from the east. In 577 AD the Irish kings of Cirencester, Bath and Gloucester were defeated by the Saxon King Caewlin of Wessex at Dyrham and southern Gloucestershire entered the Saxon sphere of influence. An independent Saxon kingdom called the Hwicce emerged, covering all of Gloucestershire, Oxfordshire, and southern Worcestershire and Warwickshire.

For the next two centuries England was split into a patchwork of minor kingdoms, with three in particular, Wessex, Northumberland and Mercia, vying for dominance. The Hwicce was left as a buffer state between Saxon England and the

Welsh, until in 757 AD it came under the control of King Offa of Mercia. Offa was a statesman of international renown, and the first Saxon to truly claim to rule all of England. He unified most of the country under a single ruler, and came to an uneasy peace with the Welsh, demarking his western frontier with a great earthwork, Offa's Dyke (walk 5).

Roman Britain had been Christian, but the Saxons were pagan, whose advance drove Christianity westwards, into Wales and Ireland. Welsh missionaries returned to England, and the Hwicce became formally Christian around 600 AD. When St Augustine arrived in Kent to re-convert England to Christianity, Gloucestershire was already Christian. In 603 AD Augustine met Welsh bishops at Aust in Gloucestershire in an abortive attempt to bring the Celtic church under the dominance of Rome. The influence of the Celtic church remained strong in Gloucestershire for many more decades, centred on the monastery of Deerhurst (walk 6).

Throughout the 9th and 10th centuries Gloucestershire was a front line in the defence of Saxon England from successive waves of Danish invaders. In 877 AD the Danes made Gloucester their base against King Alfred of Wessex, before being ejected. In 1000 AD Gloucester and Winchcombe were made the centres of two separate shires organised to combat a second wave of Danish invaders, and it was near Deerhurst that the Danish King Cnut (or Canute) was given the English crown in 1016 (walk 6).

There was little resistance to the Norman Conquest within Gloucestershire. Tewkesbury closed its gates to William the Conqueror, and was laid to waste. The Bishop of Worcester, into whose Diocese Gloucester fell, supported William the Conqueror, and under his influence resistance ceased. The county was still a border zone, with the Wye valley the logical defensible frontier. The Forest of Dean was incorporated into Gloucestershire, and two huge castles, Chepstow and Monmouth, were built to control the Wye. The Forest itself was declared a Royal Forest, and the right of hunting in it, as well as the precious iron ore reserves, were made the property of the King, controlled from the castle of St Briavels (walk 7). Royal castles were also built at Gloucester and Sharpness, to further control the county.

The Conquest was essentially an aristocratic one, and did not result in any mass influx of new settlers into England. After the invasion, King William needed an army and a nobility who could be guaranteed to defend his new kingdom. He achieved both these goals by taking the land of the defeated Saxon aristocracy and parcelling it out to his supporters, in return for which they were obliged to provide knights and men-at-arms when required. Since it was a sensitive frontier area, the King retained more land in Gloucestershire in his own hands than in most other counties, but nevertheless three-quarters of the estates were given to his followers. These Norman landowners, churchmen as well as secular barons, now had a vested interest in defending their new estates, and through them, the integrity of the realm. To protect their estates, fortified dwellings were built across the county, ranging from small fortified manor houses such as Horton Court (walk 8) to great castles such as Berkeley (walk 11).

To control and tax his new kingdom, King William needed to know the holdings of each of his vassals. To provide this, the *Domesday Book* was conceived in 1085 in Gloucester, where the King was staying, and compiled the following year, providing a comprehensive catalogue of the country's wealth and resources. Most of England's wealth was based upon the land and agriculture, and Gloucestershire was particularly rich in one particular commodity, wool. Sheep had been reared on the Cotswolds since the Iron Age, but it was after the Norman Conquest that this resource started to be fully exploited. The best business brains in the Kingdom were to be found in the Church, and the monasteries and Abbeys such as Hailes Abbey (walk 9) were in the forefront in developing commercial sheep rearing. The Church owned a quarter of the land in Gloucestershire, and was soon the wealthiest landowner in the county, and the most efficient, with estates such as Ashleworth (walk 10) typical of their holdings.

As the Welsh were subdued, the County lost much of its frontier aspect, and by the 13th century Gloucestershire was a rich county. This was due largely to the trade in wool, expanding to meet demand from the cloth industry in Flanders, but also to the iron industry of the Forest of Dean. To serve the export of both wool and iron, Bristol grew as a port, overtaking Gloucester. Many fine buildings were raised: parish churches were built, Abbeys and Monasteries expanded, and many castles were expanded to become luxurious homes as well as fortifications. One such castle, Berkeley, became infamous for the murder within its walls of King Edward II in 1327 (walk 11). The prosperity of the county suffered a severe setback in 1348, when the Black Death devastated England. A quarter of the county's population died. Many villages were left deserted, whilst others grew in their place. What happened with the Ampneys (walk 12) is typical. Despite this, Gloucestershire suffered less than much of Southern England, and economic recovery was well under way by the end of the century.

By the time that demand from Flanders for raw wool declined in the mid-14th century, Gloucestershire woollen merchants were rich enough and confident enough to begin cloth manufacture. This heralded the golden age of Gloucestershire's prosperity. The cloth industry grew rapidly, cloth merchants grew wealthy, and market towns grew in size and prosperity, with many fine churches and houses being built with the profits from wool. Towns such as Chipping Campden (walk 13) still reflect the wealth generated by the woollen industry. Bristol flourished as the main port for Cotswolds wool, developing a vigorous tradition for opening and expanding new markets. This was to form the basis for the great voyages of discovery in the 15th century. Trade was spasmodically disrupted during the Wars of the Roses, but the Battle of Tewkesbury in 1471 (walk 14) secured the throne for the Yorkists, and under Edward IV trade with Europe was increased again, to the benefit of the Cotswolds and Bristol.

The theologian William Tyndale was born and spent his early years in Gloucestershire (walk 15). He translated the Bible into English, thus allowing the ordinary man to read the scriptures for himself. Whilst Henry VIII's break with the Pope was for dynastic and political reasons, namely his need to divorce his first wife, Tyndale's writings provided the King with the intellectual justification for the Reformation of the Church in England. One of the results of that Reformation was the Dissolution of the great monastic buildings, and between 1538-9 the Abbeys of Hailes (walk 9), Tewkesbury (walk 14) and Winchcombe (walk 16), were all demolished. Eight years and five queens later, King Henry died, and his sixth wife, Catherine Parr, came to live at Sudeley Castle in Gloucestershire (walk 16), dying there the following year.

In the mid-17th century many of the county's castles, including Sudeley, were damaged or entirely demolished during and after the Civil War. At the start of that conflict, the cities of Bristol, Gloucester and Cirencester sided with Parliament, whilst many of the landed gentry declared for the king. Whilst none of the major battles of the Civil War were fought in Gloucestershire, the failure of the Royalists to capture Gloucester in 1643 is often regarded as the turning point of the war. It was essential for the King to capture the ports of Bristol and Gloucester in order to protect his rear. Bristol was taken, but despite a long and bitter siege, Gloucester held out. For the next 18 months Gloucester was used as a base from which Parliamentarian forces were able to harry the Royalists in Gloucestershire, draining their strength with the need to maintain and defend garrisons. The final battle of the Civil War occurred at Stow-on-the-Wold in September 1645, when the last Royalist army was defeated.

The county retained sympathy for the Royalist cause throughout the period of the Commonwealth. Charles II escaped after the battle of Worcester in 1651 through Gloucestershire to Bristol and the Continent, aided all the way by Royalist sympathisers. After the Restoration in 1660 Charles II lavishly rewarded his supporters, and tore down Gloucester's castle and town walls in punishment for its earlier resistance. The King did, however, also make positive attempts to reverse the damage done during the war. The Forest of Dean in particular had suffered badly from widespread deforestation during the war as well as uncontrolled mining during the reign of James I. Charles II took steps to reverse this damage, with extensive replanting of trees and formal management of the Forests resources, both the living and resources and the mineral ones (walk 17).

The 18th century brought major social and industrial changes throughout Gloucestershire. Within the Forest of Dean, iron had been extracted and worked by traditional methods that had changed little since Roman times. Charcoal, readily available in the Forest, was the fuel used for iron smelting. After the Civil War, new design coal burning blast furnaces increasingly came into use, far more productive than their charcoal fired alternatives. Fortunately the Forest was rich in coal deposits as well as iron ore, and traditional mining skills now turned increasingly to coal extraction. By the start of the 18th century, the Forest had the greatest concentration of iron foundries in England, almost entirely coal based, and the coal mining industry was flourishing around towns such as Coleford (walk 18). The former mix of open-cast mining with traditional forest-based activities was transformed into an industrial landscape. The Wye and the Severn were major arteries for coal and iron, being transported out of the Forest to the rest of England.

The wool trade was also going through a revolution. Traditionally, wool had been worked as a cottage industry, with weaving and spinning done by skilled outworkers using hand machinery in small communities such as Bibury (walk 19). The invention of the steam engine revolutionised the textile industry. Steam driven looms were much faster and more efficient, and did not rely upon expensive skilled labour. The new machinery needed purpose-built buildings to house them, near to an abundant supply of water, and so the factory system was born. The valleys of the south-west Cotswolds, around Stroud, Painswick and Wooton-under-Edge, were ideal for this, and these market towns rapidly grew into bustling industrial complexes. The skilled workers of the high Cotswolds were forced to move down into the factory towns for work, where their jobs were increasingly redundant in the face of the requirement for unskilled labour. By the mid-18th century the woollen industry was concentrated almost exclusively in one small area, and its nature transformed forever.

At the start of the 18th century Bristol was the second city and port in England. It was the major port exporting the iron and coal from the Forest of Dean and the textiles from the Cotswolds. The Severn was an artery connecting the industrial heart of England with the sea, and goods for export flowed downstream into Bristol. The city was the leading port for trade with the New World, and many Bristol merchants invested some of their wealth in the plantations of the West Indies, producing the tobacco and sugar that they then imported back into England. Bristol was transformed, as wealthy merchants built fine houses for themselves in the city and also investing in estates in the countryside around. Dodington Park (walk 20) is one of many such estates.

The 18th century also saw a darker side of Bristol's history, its involvement in the slave trade. Slaves were needed to work the plantations of the New World, and Bristol merchants were in the forefront in developing the 'Triangle' or the 'Africa Trade': textiles, iron goods and guns were transported to Africa, exchanged for slaves who were transported to the Americas where they in turn were exchanged for tobacco and sugar brought back for sale in England. A healthy profit was made at each point, much of which was then invested in the fine houses and civic buildings that are seen in Bristol today. The slave trade did not go unchallenged. The Wesley brothers, John and Charles, together with George Whitfield, had founded the Methodist movement in the 1730s, a reaction against the ceremony of the Anglican Church combined with a desire to serve Christian beliefs through practical action. The Wesleys and Whitfield travelled extensively through Gloucestershire preaching their message at vast open air meetings (see walk 21) and especially targeted Bristol and its slave trade.

Increased trade led to demands for improvements in the transport system. At the start of the 18th century roads in Gloucestershire were mostly unsurfaced, steep and narrow on the Cotswolds, rutted and muddy in the Severn Vale and the Forest of Dean. The answer was found in turnpike roads, privately funded and maintained to a good quality, on which a toll had to be paid by travellers. The first turnpike opened in Gloucestershire in 1698, and despite some local opposition, caused by resentment at the charges, most of the county's main cities were connected by turnpike to the outside world by 1800. However, the turnpikes were inadequate for moving freight. This relied upon river transport, but was subject to interruption: the Severn was known to freeze in hard winters. The national response to the demand for improved transport was the construction of canals. The first canal opened in 1761 in the Potteries, and during the next 60 years a network of canals were built all across England. In 1779 the Stroudwater Canal was built, connecting the textile mills of Stroud with the Severn and thus with Bristol and Gloucester, and in 1827 canals improved the Severn both upstream and downstream of Gloucester, thereby reviving the town's fortunes as a port. In 1789 the Thames and Severn Canal was opened, providing the first east-west link and connecting Gloucestershire and Bristol with London (walk 22).

The heyday of the canals ended with the coming of the railways. Tramways, rails along which carts were pulled by static engines, had existed for many years, particularly serving the mines of the Forest of Dean. The first railways with moveable locomotives came to Gloucestershire in 1832, and within two decades railways radiated from Bristol and Gloucester, connecting the county with all of England.

The rate of change, social and economic, accelerated during the 19th century. Whilst much of the county was still given over to agriculture, the wealth of Gloucestershire was generated by trade and by industry. The iron and coal of the Forest of Dean, the textile mills of Stroud and surroundings, the bustling ports of Bristol and Gloucester, with their rail and canal links, were now the economic heart of the county. Wealthy industrialists and merchants were buying into the landed gentry and redeveloping country estates. Members of long-established Gloucestershire families, like Warren Hastings, were using the money made through trade to renovate their family seats (walk 23). Spa towns were becoming popular, and by the early 19th century Cheltenham had developed into a highly-fashionable health resort for the gentry, aided by the coming of the railway.

But whilst industrialisation and increased trade brought prosperity to many, it also brought misery for many others. Conditions in the new textile towns, although not as grim as those in northern England, were still poor. The countryside too suffered. Increased mechanisation reduced the need for skilled labour, the increased competition of cheap food from abroad reduced demand, and after a run of poor harvests in the latter quarter of the 19th century, farming went into recession. Many workers, farmers for generations, were forced off the land, either to the industrial towns or into emigration, and long established villages fell into decay. The decline of some villages, such as Stanton and Snowshill (walk 24), was arrested by the efforts of enlightened landlords, but agriculture never recovered its former importance.

In the 20th century agriculture revived, with a return to arable farming after the two world wars. The nature of the rural population has changed, with a decline in the agricultural workforce matched by an increase in retirees, tourists and urban commuters. The population of Gloucestershire's towns has increased dramatically, with industrial development around Gloucester and Bristol. Greatly improved communications, especially the M4 and M5 have linked Gloucestershire to the rest of England as never before, aiding both industry and tourism. The county's past as remote agrarian frontier-land has now disappeared forever.

Advice to Walkers

All the walks in this collection cross countryside for at least part of their route. Although the terrain is not difficult or dangerous, it can become very wet and slippery in places, especially after a shower of rain, and walking boots or stout shoes are recommended for any of these walks. It is also recommended that you carry waterproofs, since the weather can change quickly even in Gloucestershire, and you could easily find yourself some distance away from shelter when the skies open. Remember that on some walks there may be occasional brambles, nettles or crops which scratch, so bear this in mind when deciding whether to walk in shorts.

Directions for each walk are given in the text and a sketch map included to give an outline of the route. These sketch maps are not detailed enough to navigate by, and it is strongly recommended that you carry the relevant Ordnance Survey map, in case of difficulties or in case you wish to deviate from the route. The 1:50,000 series is perfectly adequate to walk from. Although all directions are accurate at the time of writing, features do occasionally change: a hedge or tree may disappear, a stile may be replaced by a gate. By comparing the written directions with the OS map it should be perfectly possible to find the correct route even if features have occasionally altered.

All routes in this book use public rights of way or permissive footpaths when crossing private land. Again, the OS map will confirm the right of way in case of doubt. If a footpath or bridleway is shown on a current map, it is the duty of the landowner to maintain the route and you have a legal right to use it. However, it is sensible to show discretion and compromise rather than a rigid insistence on your rights: for instance, if at certain times of the year the route across an open field is not obvious or is obscured by crops, it may be better to walk around the perimeter of the field.

Consideration for others is key when walking, and at all times remember the Countryside Code laid down by the Countryside Commission:

1. **Enjoy the countryside and respect its life and work**
2. **Guard against all risk of fire**
3. **Fasten all gates**
4. **Keep your dogs under close control**
5. **Keep to public paths across farmland**
6. **Use gates and stiles to cross fences, hedges and walls**
7. **Leave livestock, crops and machinery alone**

8. Take your litter home
9. Help to keep all water clean
10. Protect wildlife, plants and trees
11. Take special care on country roads
12. Make no unnecessary noise

I have indicated where refreshments can be obtained on each walk. On a number of the walks, refreshments are only available at the beginning or end. It is therefore advisable to carry a snack, and more importantly something to drink with you, especially on the longer walks. Please note that the mention of the existence of a pub is not necessarily an endorsement of it!

Convenient car parking places have been indicated for all walks. At the time of writing, most of these were free and there is adequate parking at most spots indicated. Should you have difficulty it is far better to find a different parking spot and make your way to the start of the walk on foot, rather than causing an obstruction with your car. Most importantly, remember you are visiting a place where other people live. Do not cause inconvenience to local people by parking across access to houses, farms, fields or churches.

Walk 1

The Stone Age tomb of Belas Knap

Distance: 5 miles

Map: OS 163

Start and parking: The walk starts at the free car park in Back Lane, Winchcombe (grid ref: 024284). Winchcombe is on the B4632, six miles north of Cheltenham on the road to Stratford-upon-Avon. The car park, behind the Library, is signposted from the town centre.

Refreshments: Public houses, shops and tea rooms in Winchcombe.

Historical Background

Although man had been living in the area that is now Gloucestershire since 10,000 BC, it was not until about 3,000 BC, the 'Late Stone Age' or 'Neolithic' era, that he started to leave any permanent mark upon the landscape. The population in the whole of Britain was only 20,000, and within Gloucestershire a thousand or two at most. Neolithic man had discovered how to plant and harvest crops, especially cereals, and how to breed and husband animals. Instead of living in tents and following a moving food supply, man now built semi-permanent wooden dwellings and grew his food around them. Although they roamed the whole area to hunt and to collect wood and nuts and roots, they settled mainly upon the well-drained uplands of the Cotswolds. Here they constructed huge communal graves known as Barrows, such as Belas Knap, which have survived to this day.

Neolithic man lived in social groups based around an extended family, a family that included the dead as well as the living. It is likely that Neolithic man practiced some form of ancestor worship or at least veneration, and the dead were present to provide an on-going link between the present and the past. Huge barrows were constructed, with a building skill that ensured they would stand for 5,000 years, the most permanent structures of their own or any other age. The whole community worked together for several months to build the barrow, probably when time became available after the harvest was in. In the barrow were buried selected dead, over many centuries, the grave-

18

mound being opened and sealed again time after time. What ceremony was involved, or why certain individuals were thus interred, whilst the rest of the community went into unmarked graves, is unknown.

Barrows were built upon conspicuous airy hilltops and ridges, not only for religious reasons but also for territorial ones. Each Neolithic community had its own territory, and the visual presence of the tomb announced the long-term interconnection between a people and a specific area of land. Before the woods grew up which obscure today's sky-line, Belas Knap would have been visible for miles.

The Walk

This walk starts in the historic market town of Winchcombe, and then climbs steadily through fields on to the Cotswolds ridge, with fine views across the valley. It visits the Neolithic barrow of Belas Knap before descending again to Winchcombe, passing several sites of interest within the town itself.

- Leave the car park and turn right along Back Lane, towards the town centre.

- At the crossroads, turn right into North Street.

- Go along North Street to a T-junction. Cross the road to the inn sign (St George) and peep down the alleyway to see the ex-George Inn opposite.

Before it became private property, the George Inn was a coaching inn, but even before that it had been a hostel for pilgrims travelling to Winchcombe Abbey, which was second only to Canterbury as a destination for pilgrimage in the Middle Ages. Above the door of the inn are the initials 'R K', standing for Richard of Kidderminster, the last Abbot of Winchcombe, who died before he could witness the dissolution of the Abbey in 1539.

- Facing the George, turn right along the High Street, passing the Tourist Information Centre on the corner opposite.

- Pass through the Market Square, with its old inns and war memorial.

On the left is Dent Terrace, a row of almshouses. The first almshouses here were founded in 1573 by Lady Chandos, whose family had succeeded the Seymours as owners of Sudeley Castle (passed later in this walk) and the surrounding estates. The terrace was renovated in 1887, and at the same time the town's first regular water supply was laid on. Both deeds were the work of Emma Dent, who had inherited Sudeley Castle from her uncles and husband.

- Just past the square, turn left down Vineyard Street.

- Follow the lane across the river.

This lane was formerly known as Duck Street, since at the river there was a ducking stool

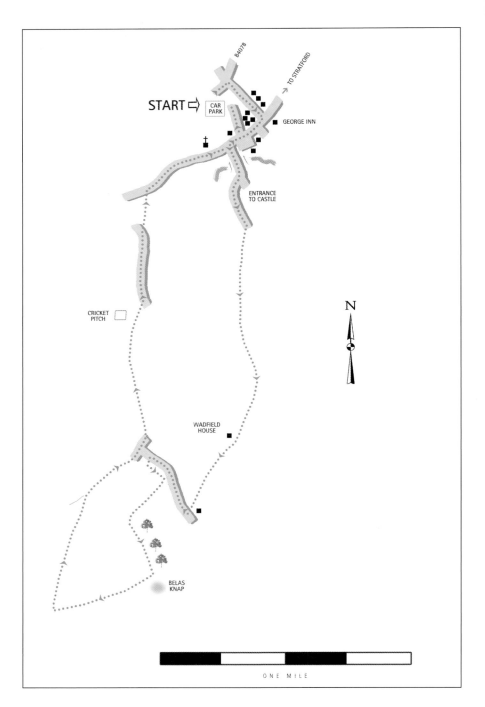

START ➡

CAR PARK

B4078

TO STRATFORD

GEORGE INN

ENTRANCE TO CASTLE

CRICKET PITCH

N

WADFIELD HOUSE

BELAS KNAP

ONE MILE

in the Middle Ages. This was a common form of punishment, whereby a 'scold', or an offensively sharp-tongued woman of the community, was tied to a stool and ducked in the river, to force her to adopt behaviour more acceptable to her neighbours.

- Continue along the lane to the entrance to Sudeley Castle, and there turn right to continue along the lane signed 'No Through Road'.

For a history of Sudeley Castle see walk 16.

- Follow the lane for 350 yards, and then turn right through a kissing gate, signed 'Belas Knap'.

- Go half-left across the field to pass a telegraph pole. Continue the same line of advance to a stile in the middle of the hedge ahead.

- Cross the stile and go half-right across a second field, still the same line of advance, to a stile beside the middle one of three telegraph poles opposite.

- Cross this stile and maintain your line of advance across a third field to a footbridge in the far corner.

- Cross the footbridge and climb steps. Continue ahead along the side of a fourth field, a hedge on your right.

- Follow the footpath as it turns right over a stile in the hedge, and then immediately turn left up the next field, the hedge now on your left.

- Follow the field boundary around to the right to a stile.

- Cross the stile and continue along an enclosed footpath, to reach a house.

This house is called Wadfield House, and takes its name from woad, a plant used as the basis for blue and black dyes. Woad was a valuable crop used in Winchcombe's cloth industry and grown here until the end of the 19th century, but its uses as a dye go much farther back in time. The Iron Age Britons who opposed the Romans were renowned for painting their bodies with woad as a traditional warpaint that had been used for intimidating enemies for many centuries. Traces of body paint have been found in Neolithic tombs, and woad was almost certainly used by the Stone Age builders of nearby Belas Knap.

- Keep ahead along the side of a field, a hedge on your right, to reach a farm drive.

- Keep ahead up the drive, eventually passing to the right of cottages, to reach a drive leading up to a lane.

- Turn right along the lane for a quarter of a mile. Once over the crest of a hill, ignore a footpath to your right but 300 yards later, turn left over a stile, signed 'Belas Knap'.

- Follow a broad path steeply uphill through trees.

- Leave the trees via a kissing gate and turn sharp left along the edge of a field, woods on your left hand.

- Follow the field boundary around to the right and uphill to a kissing gate in the top corner.

- Go through the kissing gate and continue with the wood on your left hand.

These woods are called Humblebee How. The name is not an association with the insect, but derives from 'Hamol Hoh', meaning 'sacred hillside'.

- Follow the path through the edge of woodland for quarter of a mile to a kissing gate leading to Belas Knap. A path circles the tumulus, allowing it to be viewed from all sides.

Belas Knap is a long barrow, or communal burial chamber, dating from approximately 3000 BC. It marked a second-stage development in the design of long barrows. Initially, barrows were of the type known as 'transept gallery', with a long central corridor leading from an elaborate portal, and with side chambers leading off the corridor in which the dead were buried. (Hetty Pegler's Tump, seen on walk 2, is an example of this type of Barrow.) However, tombs became subject to the attention of grave robbers, and the answer was the 'false portal' chambered barrow, of which Belas Knap is a fine example. An elaborate door, actually leading nowhere, was built at one end and then sealed, whilst the tomb was actually entered through secret doors located elsewhere. Inside, chambers still led off a central corridor. A third stage of development was eventually to see the side chambers randomly placed and sealed, in a further effort to deter thieves.

The tomb complex of corridor and side chambers was built of large slabs of Oolite, placed upright and then capped with flat stones as a roof. It was then buried under an earthen mound. Belas Knap was originally 200ft long, 80ft long, and 13½ft high. The elaborate false entrance was built of Stonesfield slate, in a style that was the precursor of modern dry-stone walling. Unfortunately much of the mound has been restored using modern materials, which have buried the original.

The tomb was used for many centuries after its original construction, 38 bodies in all

Belas Knap tumulus.

have been found in Belas Knap, both men and women, of all ages, including children. They had been buried at different times over many centuries, some with grave goods buried with them. As the land became exhausted by the primitive farming methods of the day, the people would move to new land a little further away. Eventually the barrow was too far from the tribe for it to be of practical use, and it was abandoned. However, Romano-British pottery has been found near the false entrance, suggesting Belas Knap may have been reused much later still. 'Belas Knap' means Beacon Hill, a name given to the site long after its initial use had finished.

- With your back to the false northern entrance to the tumulus, turn left and cross steps in the wall ahead.

- Keep straight on along the edge of a field, a wall on your right hand.

- At the end of the field, at a Cotswolds Way fingerpost, turn right along a track.

- Follow the track, soon tarmacked, for half a mile, to reach a T-junction.

- Bear right to continue in the same general direction, views of Winchcombe off to your left. Follow the track for another 300 yards to reach a junction with a road.

- Immediately upon joining the road, go left up steps and over a stile into a field.

- Bear a quarter-right downhill, aiming for a waymark post in mid-field 100 yards ahead.

- At the post go quarter-left downhill, now aiming for a white-topped post 200 yards ahead.

- From the white-topped post keep straight on to pass an isolated tree directly ahead and then to a signpost directly behind the tree.

- Cross a stile beside the signpost on to a drive and turn right.

- Follow the drive past a cricket field and out to a road.

- Turn left along the road for 500 yards, passing houses on your left. Just after Lark Rise on the left, where the road bends left, turn right through a kissing gate.

- Turn left and follow the fence on your left around the edge of the field, gardens over the fences and hedges on your left. In the bottom of the field go through a kissing gate and over a footbridge.

- Go up a tarmacked path to a road and turn right.

- Go along the road, passing Tobacco Close on the left.

Tobacco was brought back from America by Sir Walter Raleigh, and from 1619 was grown in Winchcombe, one of the earliest sites where tobacco was grown commercially in England. As the tobacco habit grew, and increasing quantities of the plant were imported, it became an extremely profitable crop to grow, since it escaped import duty. Under pressure from the big tobacco importers of Bristol, the government banned the growing of tobacco in England in 1652. This was deeply resented by the small-holders of Winchcombe, who ignored the ban. Bailiffs sent to destroy the crop were bloodily repulsed by villagers in the 'Tobacco Riots', and troops had to be sent in to enforce the law. Despite this, the law was still ignored and tobacco continued to be grown here until 1690, when cheap foreign imports finally made it uneconomic.

● Continue along the road, ex-weavers' cottages on the left.

Weaving was the principal industry of Winchcombe for 500 years. 'Winchcombe jerseys' were known throughout Europe at the start of the Tudor era. Weavers were self-employed, usually living in tied cottages above a ground floor workshop, where they wove their landlord's wool (see walk 19). Weaving declined in the 17th century, when the focus of the cloth trade started to move to the nearby valley-towns such as Stroud, where water was readily available to drive the new technology.

● Follow the road to the church.

The parish church of St Peters was built from the profits of the local woollen industry. It was begun around 1465, later than most Cotswold 'wool churches', financed by the combined efforts of the Abbey and the local wool merchants. One such, Sir Ralph Botelier, is depicted as one of the churches many elaborate gargoyles. Inside the church is beautiful rood screen, elaborately decorated with wood carvings including the Winchcombe imp amongst more traditional designs. There is also an altar cloth thought to have been embroidered by Catherine of Aragon on display.

In Queen's Square on the right is Jacobean House, built in 1619 and attributed to Inigo Jones, later the home of the Dent family, leading merchants and benefactors in the town, and subsequent owners of Sudeley Castle (see walk 16).

● Continue along the road and along the market square.

Winchcombe Abbey once stood behind the high wall on the left. Winchcombe was the capital of King Kenulf, who founded the Abbey in 811 AD, in memory of his son Kenelm. Kenelm, a seven-year-old boy designated by Kenulf as his heir, was murdered by his own sister Quendrida, who herself had aspirations on the crown. An existing nunnery, founded 25 years earlier by Kenulf's predecessor Offa, was redeveloped as an elaborate Abbey, and given to the Benedictines to tend.

The Abbey grew to great wealth, partly by shrewd investment in land and sheep rearing, and partly due to Kenelm's elevation to sainthood, which made Winchcombe into a place of pilgrimage second only to Canterbury. In 1539 the Abbey was confiscated under the Dissolution, much of its land contributing to the fortunes of Lord Seymour of Sudeley. Within a few years nothing remained of the Abbey, even its stones being removed to build local houses. The stone coffins of Kenulf and Kenelm did survive however, and are today in St Peter's Church.

● At the end of the square, turn left into Cowl Lane. Follow the lane for 150 yards and then turn left back into the car park.

Walk 2

Uley Bury: hill forts defend the land in the Iron Age

Distance: 3.5 miles

Map: OS 162

Start and parking: This walk starts at the church in Uley (grid ref: 792986). Uley is on the B4066, two miles east of Dursley and six miles west of Stroud. There is ample parking in the wide main street of Uley, either just to the east of the church or in the village centre, but park with consideration for local people.

Refreshments: Shops and public houses in Uley.

Historical Background

From around 2000 BC until 1000 BC, the steady increase in population caused Bronze Age man to spread from the Wessex Downs, along the course of the Thames valley, and to settle the eastern slopes of the Cotswolds. But Gloucestershire remained thinly populated and the thickly forested Severn valley and Forest of Dean were shunned. After 1000 BC the climate across the British Isles deteriorated, becoming colder and wetter. The rising water-table made the soil of the Cotswolds too heavy and wet for growing crops, and many of the higher areas were abandoned, and their inhabitants moved down into the valleys of the Thames and Severn. At the same time the population had increased dramatically, and competition for the available arable land increased.

This movement and increase in population coincided with the increased use of iron for tools and for weapons. Iron was easier to work than bronze, and iron ore was much more accessible. Consequently, iron weapons rapidly became readily available, and were used to settle the ever more frequent conflicts over land. The first Iron Age settlers spread into Gloucestershire from around 550 BC onwards, entering from the Severn estuary and up the Thames valley, and with their superior weapons they gradually ousted the existing Bronze Age communities. For protection, families and tribes coalesced into loose confederations and petty kingdoms, headed by a ruling élite versed in the ways of war.

Once they had seized the land, the new Iron Age immigrants set about defending it. A line of strong hill forts were built along the crest of the Cotswolds, where natural features could be re-inforced to create sites that were easy to defend. These forts offered protection to the families and homesteads living and working the fertile land of the Severn valley and its tributaries. They were built to provide refuge in times when inter-tribal rivalry boiled over into armed conflict, and to overawe rivals with a dramatic symbol of the power and prestige of the tribe.

Uley Bury is one of the finest examples of a hill fort in Gloucestershire. It was built by the earliest Iron Age settlers to penetrate the region, around 550 BC, a tribe whose name is now lost. It remained their tribal home for 450 years, until they in turn were driven out by even more powerful newcomers, the Dobunni.

The Walk

This short walk starts with a steady ascent through trees to reach the Neolithic burial mound of Hetty Pegler's Tump, and then returns mostly on the flat, through an attractive wooded section of the Cotswolds Way to the spectacular hill fort of Uley Bury.

Uley is an old cloth-making village. As early as 1608 it is recorded that three cloth merchants employed 29 weavers to turn their raw wool into broadcloth. Like most of the wool manufacturing villages in the Cotswolds, Uley was specialised, in Uley's case producing the blue cloth used for the uniforms of the British Navy. During the 17th and 18th centuries Uley was a hive of activity, but the weavers were paid a pittance and formed illegal and secret societies, the forerunner of later trade unions, in order to fight to improve their conditions.

- With your back to the church, turn left along the B4066, passing the Old Crown public house and the village green on your right.

St Giles' Church was built in 1857 by the architect S.S. Teulon, who also built the nearby Tyndale Monument (see walk 15). The interior of St Giles' was influenced by the Oxford Movement, which advocated a return to High Church ceremony.

- Continue along the pavement on the left-hand side of the road, passing a side turn on the right and continuing up Crawley Hill.

- After a quarter of a mile reach the first house on the right (Crawley House). Go into the unmade track to the right (downhill) side of the house, and cross over a waymarked stile on the right.

- Turn left and go down the side of the field, a fence and hedge on your left.

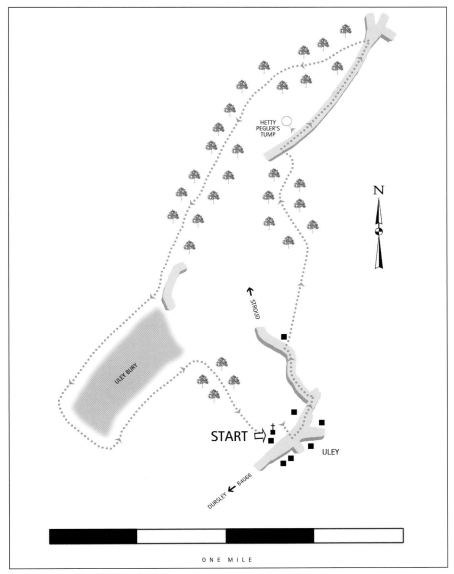

ONE MILE

The bulk of Uley Bury hill fort dominates the skyline to your left.

● At the field bottom cross a stream and continue uphill, a hedge still on your right. Aim for a waymarked stile soon visible in the top corner of the field.

● Cross the stile and maintain your line of advance up the next field, the hedge still on your left.

- At the summit of the field, just before the hedge starts to descend, bear left on a footpath into the trees.

- Cross a stile and go over a cross track, to keep more or less ahead up a broad track climbing into woods.

- In 20 yards ignore a right turn downhill but continue uphill on the main (left hand) track.

- At a T-junction at the top of the slope, bear right along a wide flat track, until you reach metal gates at the top of a final slope.

- Go through the gates on to the road and turn right.

- This road is not over busy, but cars travel fast along it, and it is recommended that you use the grass verge on the other side of the road. Walk with care along the road for 200 yards, and then turn left at a sign for 'Uley Long Barrow'.

Uley tumulus is a long barrow of a type known as transepted gallery-graves. A later, and more elaborate, example of this design of long barrow can be seen at Belas Knap (walk 1). It is 180 feet long, and 90 feet wide, and rises to a height of 10 foot. A central passage (the gallery) runs down the long axis of the tomb, with three side chambers (the transepts) leading off from the passage. The barrow was dry-stone built, with a stone retaining wall around it, and the whole covered with an earthen mound. It was first constructed around 3000 BC and was used as a communal burial mound for the next 1,200 years, with the tomb regularly being re-opened and fresh bodies interred, 34 skeletons have been found

Uley Bury hill fort.

within the tomb. Why only certain members of the community were selected to be interred within long barrows, whilst the rest were buried with less ceremony elsewhere, is unknown.

Every few decades the communities that built the long barrows would move their settlements a few miles, once they had exhausted the land, and over the centuries the barrows became further and further away from where the people now lived, and so eventually were abandoned.

There is a cultural link between the barrows such as Uley and Belas Knap, found on the Cotswolds, and those found in Brittany, suggesting that there was migration by sea across the English Channel and up the Bristol Channel to the Severn estuary. Long barrows served not only as graves but also as territorial boundary markers, and are usually found upon high, visible places. Before the woods grew up on the slope below Uley barrow it would have been visible for miles across the Severn valley.

Uley tumulus is also known as Hetty Pegler's Tump, named after Hester, the wife of the local 17th century landowner.

- After visiting the long barrow, return to the road and turn left to resume your previous direction. Continue along the road for 400 yards and then, just before a road junction, turn left on to a footpath (signed 'Cotswolds Way').

- Follow the stony track downhill through trees.

- Where the path divides, keep to the upper path. Follow this path, which soon levels out.

- Where steps come in from the right, turn left uphill through a horse barrier. Follow the narrow path along the slope.

- Eventually pass through a second horse barrier and climb with the path to a gateway on your left (and a wooden bench on your right).

- Go through the wooden gate and just before the road turn right through a metal gate. Follow the track to the entrance of Uley Bury hill fort.

Uley Bury hill fort is one of the finest examples of a 'promontory' fort in England. It was built by enclosing the end of a spur, a building technique common in the Iron Age Cotswolds, but rare elsewhere in the British Isles. You are now passing through the ramparts that cut off the neck of the promontory, and going through a gateway into the fort itself.

- At a 'No Rubbish Tipping' sign, go forward for a few yards to the edge of a huge open field.

In front of you is the vast central enclosure of Uley Bury, covering some 38 acres. The natural defensive position, upon the end of a steep-sided spur, was reinforced by the construction of a double earthen rampart with an intervening ditch around the perimeter. The outer rampart would have been further strengthened with a wooden palisade on top, creating a well-nigh impregnable position. There were three entrances through the ramparts, in the north, south and eastern corners.

Uley was built around 550 BC by early Iron Age settlers. Whilst many small hill forts, such as Brackenbury just to the south (see walk 15), were built merely to provide emergency shelter, Uley was in continual use. It acted as an administrative and commercial centre for the locality, and the flat central enclosure would have been filled with the huts of the regular inhabitants, as well as stockades and temporary accommodation for passing travellers. The bulk of the tribe would have lived outside the fort, either on the Cotswold ridge or in the fertile valleys below the fort, and there would have been plenty of open space within the fort to shelter the scattered farmers and there livestock if trouble materialised. Uley was continually occupied throughout the Iron Age and was eventually taken over by immigrants belonging to the Dobunni tribe (see walk 3). It was a tribal centre for the Dobunni throughout the Roman era, with Roman coins from the first to fourth centuries found here.

● Return to the sign. Facing the sign, turn right and follow the track around the top of the ramparts.

The inner rampart is to your left. To your right is the outer rampart, with a steep drop to the valley below. Between the two, where you are walking, was a deep ditch. The last 2,000 years have mellowed these fortifications, although even today they are still impressive. When they were first built, the ramparts would have been far higher and steeper, and the ditch deeper. The outer rampart would have been topped with a wooden palisade as a further defence. Any attacker would have needed to scale the steep slope, under constant missile attack from the defenders above, fought their way across the defended palisade, only to find themselves in a deep ditch, under further attack from defenders on the inner rampart.

● Ignore a stile to the right in 500 yards but continue along the ramparts. Turn left with the ramparts and go along the southern face of the fort, the view now more open.

From here it is easy to see the double ramparts ahead of you, and to appreciate their defensive position atop the steep slopes of the spur.

● At the next corner, where the path around the ramparts turns left again, climb on to the mounds to your right.

Below you is the southern gate giving access into Uley Bury. The gates were the most vulnerable part of the hill forts, and consequently the most heavily defended. A complex maze of defensive breastworks can be seen below you, where the narrow entrance passageway wound its way between high, sheer-sided ramparts. The passage would have been blocked in one or more places by moveable barriers of heavy logs when necessary. Not only was the gateway easy to defend, but it was also overlooked and commanded by more defenders on the ramparts above, where you are now standing.

Looking the other way the flat open interior of the fort and its surrounding ring of ramparts can clearly be appreciated.

- From the southern gate, continue around the fort, keeping the drop to your right and the inner ramparts on your left. Eventually go sharp left around the next corner of the fort.

- Thirty yards past the corner, turn sharp right downhill at a bridleway sign.

- Go steeply downhill. At a cross track beside a ruined gate and stile, keep straight on along the main path.

- Ignore all side turns and continue to descend steadily through the trees to reach a gate.

- Go through the gate and follow a distinct path around the side of the hill, maintaining your previous line of advance.

- As soon as Uley church comes into view directly ahead, look for a faint path leading off right down the slope. Follow this path, which becomes clearer as you descend, and aims just to the right of the corner of a hedge seen ahead.

- Follow the path to a stile beside a gate. Cross the stile and keep ahead for 10 yards, then turn left into a tree lined footpath (signed 'To church' at the time of writing, although the sign looks in imminent danger of disappearing).

- Follow the footpath along the side of the churchyard and out on to the road.

Walk 3

Minchinhampton: capital city in the Iron Age

Distance: 4 miles

Map: OS 162

Start and parking: The walk starts from the market square, Minchinhampton (grid ref: 873008). Minchinhampton is on a network of minor roads, three miles south of Stroud. It can be reached from the A46 at Nailsworth, the A419 at Brownshill, or from Stroud itself. There is a free car park off Friday Street, Minchinhampton, just behind the market square, or roadside parking in and around the town.

Refreshments: Public houses, shops and tea rooms in Minchinhampton.

Historical Background
Around 100 BC a new wave of settlers entered Gloucestershire. These were the Dobunni, part of the Belgae, a people who lived in northern mainland Europe and gradually spread across the sea to Britain. The Dobunni were an advanced people compared to the existing inhabitants of Gloucestershire, having not only technologically superior weapons but also a far more sophisticated social organisation and system of trade. They arrived up the Severn estuary, and soon established their dominance, peacefully assimilating as many of the existing tribes as they could, conquering by force those they had to. Very rapidly the land of the Dobunni encompassed all the area of modern Gloucestershire east of the Severn, as well as Oxfordshire and much of Worcestershire and Warwickshire. The capital of the Dobunni tribe was at Minchinhampton.

Around 10 AD, under pressure from their neighbours to the east, the powerful Catuvellauni tribe, the kingdom was divided into two. The southern part of the Dobunni lands continued to be ruled from Minchinhampton, by King Corio-something (his full name being lost to history), a client of the Catuvellauni. The northern part was ruled by the more independent King Bobuocus, who built a new capital at Begendon (near present-day Cirencester).

When the Romans invaded in 43 AD, the Dobunni under King Bobuocus rapidly offered a formal surrender to the Roman Emperor Claudius. The other half of the kingdom supported the Catuvellauni in their resistance to the invader, but were rapidly outflanked and defeated. To control the conquered territories in Gloucestershire, the Romans built a city, Corinium (later called Cirencester) to act as an administrative centre, just five miles south of the capital of the friendlier Dobunni, Begendon. Very soon the economic and political heart of Gloucestershire was focused upon Corinium and Begendon, and Minchinhampton faded from the sight of history.

The Walk

This flat, easy walk starts in Minchinhampton and goes around the Minchinhampton plateau, where there are many remains of the Iron Age city still to be seen, and fine views are afforded over the surrounding countryside.

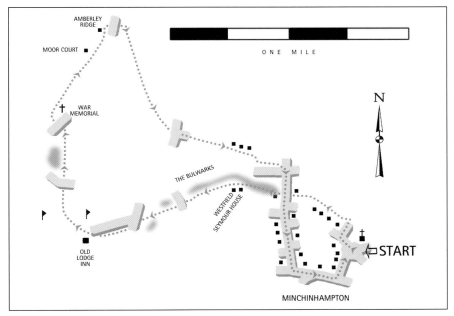

- Make your way into the Market Square, just south of the church in Minchinhampton.

In the 13th century Minchinhampton was an important market town, with its own weekly market and annual five-day fair. It was already becoming a leading cloth-making town. Cloth making was still a cottage industry, with individual craftsmen and their families working from their own homes. Minchinhampton flourished as a wool town until the onset of the Industrial Revolution, which in the Cotswolds centred on towns in the nearby valleys such as Stroud, where plentiful water power was available to drive the new machinery. By the 19th century Minchinhampton had become a dormitory, with skilled workers going down the hill into Stroud each day to find work.

- With your back to the 17th-century market hall, cross the square, passing the war memorial, and go along Bell Lane, passing the church on your right.

The church of Holy Trinity dates from the 12th century, although it was largely rebuilt in 1842. The 14th-century spire was reduced to its present height in 1543, and topped with pinnacles and crenellations. The transept still shows original 14th-century masonry.

- Follow the churchyard wall around to the right, to reach the common.

- Turn left along a tarmacked path (marked 'Private Road'), a wall on your left. Follow the path until the tarmac ends, and then keep ahead along a clear grassy path, the wall still on your right.

- Bear left with the wall and the grassy path, to reach a road.

- Cross the road and continue along the wall, following a path along the top of the Bulwarks.

The earthen ramparts known as The Bulwarks were raised in the first century BC and surrounded an area of 590 acres, most of the top of the Minchinhampton plateau. The outside was to the left as you are now standing, the surrounded interior area to the right. Two thousand years ago, they would have been much higher than today, rising almost sheer to a height of 12 feet. Outside the rampart was a deep ditch (the remains can be seen on the left), a further obstacle to any assault.

Within the ramparts was the capital of the Dobunni from around 90 BC until 47 AD. The population was huge by Iron Age standards, with several thousand permanent inhabitants. The area within the ramparts would have been filled with wooden buildings, mostly one-storey but often very large, interspersed with cattle pens, market gardens where individual families grew their own vegetables, stables and warehouses for traders, forges and workshops.

Many of the inhabitants were engaged in agriculture, with the well-drained land on the plateau outside the ramparts cultivated for crops, and also used for grazing cattle and goats. However, a sizeable proportion of the population worked at more urban activities. Minchinhampton was the trading centre for 30 miles around, at which local produce was exchanged for exotic imports from the rest of Britain and the continent. Corn, cattle, hides and hounds, gold, silver and iron were all exported to Europe. Commerce was conducted not by barter but by using a cash economy, based upon bronze or gold coins, or iron ingots of a fixed weight. Coins were minted in Minchinhampton, which was also the political capital of the area, where the Kings of the Dobunni lived and held court, receiving ambassadors from all the other Kingdoms of Britain and also from their ethnic cousins in Gaul (modern France and Belgium).

Minchinhampton's strong ramparts were strengthened still further in 43 AD, in preparation for resisting the advancing Romans. In the event, the Dobunni and their allies

Iron-age ramparts at Minchinhampton.

were defeated piecemeal in a series of skirmishes, and Minchinhampton surrendered without ever being assaulted.

- Just before the road, leave the ramparts and bear left. Follow the path, a wall on your left hand.

- Pass the gate of Seymour House, and then of Westfield. Continue along a broad grassy track across the common, leaving the wall and heading towards a wall and trees on the far side of the open common.

This area was called Westfield, and was in fact the site of one of three huge medieval fields located around Minchinhampton. Crop rotation was practiced, with one field lying fallow every year. Each villager owned strips of land in each of the fields, scattered across the fields to ensure an equal share of good and poor land.

- Cross a road and walk straight on past Windmill House.

- Keep ahead, a wall on your left and ramparts on your right.

- Just before the wall starts to curve left, bear right through a gap through the ramparts.

- Keep ahead to meet the road at a prominent signboard for Old Lodge Inn.

- Cross the road and walk along the verge of the drive leading to Old Lodge Inn.

Until the Stroud to Cirencester turnpike opened in the early 19th century, Minchinhampton was the meeting point of several busy stagecoach routes. The Old Lodge is a 16th century coaching inn dating from that era.

- Keep along the access road to pass Old Lodge Inn on your left, the golf course on your immediate right. Where the access road turns left behind the building, bear half-right across the common, aiming to the left of a clearly visible white marker pole.

- Pass the pole and maintain your line of advance down the slope. BEWARE of golf balls; the right of way shares the common with a golf fairway here. Pass between two single bushes to reach a cross-track.

- Turn right along the broad grassy track, trees and bushes on your left and the open common on your right.

- There is soon a wall off on your left hand. Maintain your line of advance, passing a 'green' on your left to reach a road at the point where it bends right and descends sharply.

- Cross the road and keep straight on along a footpath through earthworks.

These earthworks are the ramparts of Amberley Fort, an Iron Age fortification that pre-dates the growth of Minchinhampton as the Dobunni capital. It was small, strongly defensible but unlikely to have been regularly garrisoned, being instead an emergency shelter for local tribesmen in times of emergency. Several natural routeways lead down from the plateau at this point, and the fort was later incorporated into the western gateway of the Dobunni capital.

- DO NOT follow the path that stays to a prominent edge, but instead follow one that veers slightly right, aiming between the right-hand houses seen ahead.

- Follow the path to a road, the Celtic cross of a war memorial visible opposite.

- Cross the road, pass the war memorial and follow the footpath ahead, which very soon curves right along the edge of the common.

- Follow the clear path, trees down to the left and the road up to the right.

- Soon a wall is reached on your left. Keep ahead along the wall to reach the gates of Moor Court.

- Cross the drive and keep ahead along a clear path to reach the gates of Amberley Ridge.

- Turn right up to the road. Cross the road and walk straight ahead for 10 yards, passing a large single tree on your left hand, to reach a faint grassy cross path.

- Turn right along the path, which soon becomes more distinct as it swings left around the hillside.

On the crest of the common you can just see a raised mound. This is a stone-age long barrow, called since the 18th century 'Whitfield's Tump'. In 1743 George Whitfield, one of the founders of Methodism, preached here to a crowd of 20,000, despite having been physically attacked only a few hours earlier in the market square by people opposed to his revolutionary religious views. Like Wesley, Whitfield believed in simple adherence to Christian teachings combined with a practical application of Christian beliefs. Nearby Bristol and its slave trade was a particular target of his. By 1743 he had split with Wesley over doctrinal differences (see walk 21).

- Pass a thornbush-filled quarry on your right and follow the path, now wider, across a cross track, and continue ahead.

- Follow the path above houses on your left, to a road, at a sign for Burleigh.

- Cross the road and keep ahead along a No Through Road opposite.

- Where the road bends sharply left at the end of a row of houses, keep straight on, soon with a high wall on your left.

- Keep ahead along a tarmacked drive, a wall and houses on your left, to reach a main road.

- Turn left along the main road for 200 yards to a crossroads, and turn right along Dr Brown's Road.

- Follow Dr Brown's Road through the ramparts. Continue along the road for a quarter of a mile, passing side roads to right and left, to reach a T-junction.

- Turn left and follow the road for 350 yards, to reach High Street on your left. Turn left and follow High Street back to the market square.

Walk 4

Chedworth: the Romans in Gloucestershire

Distance: 4 miles

Map: OS 163

Start and parking: The walk starts from the Seven Tuns public house in Chedworth (grid ref: 052121). Chedworth is on a minor road on the north side of the A429 (Fosse Way), 13 miles south of Stow-in-the-Wold and six miles north of Cirencester. The turn-off is clearly marked both for 'Chedworth' and 'Roman Villa', but follow the signs to the village itself and not the villa. The Seven Tuns is next to the church in Chedworth, (avoid going to Lower Chedworth). There is roadside parking around the church and pub.

Refreshments: Public house at start and end of walk, in Chedworth.

Historical Background

The initial war aim for the Roman invasion in 43 AD was the subjugation of southern Britain, and within four years this had been achieved. By 47 AD the frontier of Roman Britain was a line from the Wash to the Severn. A military road, later called the Fosse Way, ran from Lincoln to Exeter, with garrison towns established along its route. Initially Gloucestershire was a frontier zone, with Gloucester and Cirencester garrison towns. Forts such as Kingsholm housed foreign troops from as far away as Greece and Switzerland. By 70 AD, the invasion was moving northwards, and Gloucestershire was handed over to a civilian administration, whose aim was to romanise the population. The Romans had no prejudice against race or colour and easily assimilated new populations into the empire, and part of the genius of the Romans was in getting local inhabitants to accept the benefits of Roman civilization and thus have a stake in preserving the Empire.

The area of Gloucestershire on the eastern slopes of the Cotswolds had been important agriculturally in pre-Roman times, and the Romans set about developing this resource, partly by introducing new agricultural methods and partly by providing access to a huge, stable market. At one level peasant communities, villages and simple farmsteads, continued to function much as they had done before the invasion, but superimposed upon these were new communities based upon villas. An elaborate house provided the administrative centre of a large farm. It was surrounded by outbuildings such as barns and stables and the dwellings of farm workers, and was in the centre of orchards and fields. The villas were built close to the Roman roads, which provided access to markets. These villas provided the hub of Roman-style agriculture in Gloucestershire, and were usually owned, not by foreigners, but by native Britons who had seen the benefits of the Roman system and had embraced the Roman way of life.

The villas came later to Gloucestershire than to the rest of southern England, a reflection of its frontier status, but today there are over 50 known villas in the county. The finest example is to be seen at Chedworth.

The Walk

This walk starts by climbing out of the village of Chedworth, with splendid views back across the valley. It then goes through fields and rolling woodland, on field paths and tracks, and one quiet lane, before visiting Chedworth Roman villa.

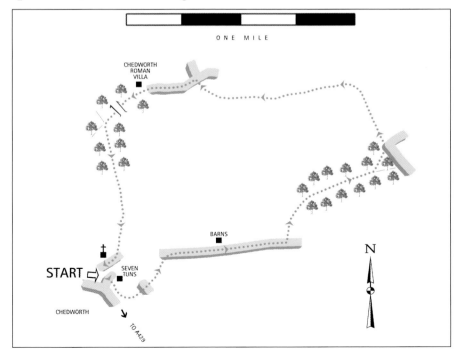

The village of Chedworth has always been centred on the hollow now occupied by the Seven Tuns, where a spring of fresh water bubbles out of the rock all year round and provided a fresh water supply for villagers and livestock alike. The present public house dates from 1610, although there was an inn on this site long before that.

- Standing facing the Seven Tuns public house, go through a gateway immediately to the right of the pub, marked as Footpath.

- Bear left, passing stables on your left hand, to a stile beside a gate ahead.

- Cross the stile and keep ahead along the top of the field, a wall close on your right hand, to reach a stile in the corner of the field, 10 yards to the left of a gate.

- Go over the stile, and 5 yards later, turn left over a second stile into woodland.

- Go straight ahead over the raised embankment (the course of an ex-railway), and once over the crest, bear left downhill to a stile.

- Cross the stile and descend some steps into a field. Keep ahead down the field, a hedge on your left.

- Cross a stile at the bottom of the field. Go over a small footbridge and bear left, to climb an enclosed footpath to a lane.

- Cross the lane and keep ahead up a footpath, passing cottages on your right, to a gate.

- Go through the gate and up the field, a wall on your right, to reach another gate.

- Go through this second gate and keep ahead along an enclosed footpath, passing through two more gates to reach a lane.

- Turn right along the lane. In quarter of a mile pass barns on your left.

- Continue along the lane for another 600 yards, to where a footpath crosses the road (footpath signs point to each side). Turn left through the rightmost of two adjacent gates into a field.

- With your back to the gate, keep ahead across the field, aiming for a tree in mid-field, which soon comes into sight.

- Pass the tree on your right hand and maintain your line of advance down the field, to reach a footpath post at the edge of woodland.

- Follow the broad path through the woods, descending gently, for almost half a mile, until a faint cross track is reached. (Look for the yellow waymark post obscured in brambles to the left of the path.) Turn left up the cross track.

- (If you miss the turn you will shortly end up on a road. Here turn left for 150 yards to a sharp right-angled bend in the road, where you will rejoin the walk at a track marked 'Private Road, footpath only'.)

- After 30 yards, at a T-junction, turn right along a clearer track.

Chedworth Roman Villa.

- In another 20 yards, at a waymark sign, turn left along a narrower footpath.

- Follow the footpath across a cross-track and soon descend to reach a road.

- Turn left for 15 yards. Where the road makes a right-angled turn to the right, keep straight on along a stony track, marked 'Private Road, footpath only'.

- Follow this wooded track for a mile, to eventually pass through green gates on to a road.

- Turn left up the road, signed 'Roman Villa only'. In 100 yards ignore a Bridleway sign to your left but continue up the road to reach Chedworth Roman Villa.

Chedworth Villa was built at the head of a small valley, protected on three sides from the weather, and with a supply of continuous water. When built, there would have been fewer trees around the villa, and they would have been deciduous varieties, not the conifers seen today. To cope with the slope, the foundations were built on a series of level platforms, and thus the villa was built on different levels. Initially there were three separate blocks, with the main house on the upper, western slope.

When it was first built, around 120 AD, the villa was very much the hub of a working farm, and although it was later rebuilt and somewhat enlarged, it remained a utilitarian building for the next two hundred years. The farm was based upon a mixed economy, with some land given over to arable farming, mainly cereals, but with most money being made from stock raising. Cattle were kept for milk, cheese, meat, hides and glue. Goats and sheep were raised primarily for wool, which was exported throughout the Empire. Vegetables, mainly root crops, and fruit such as apples, plums and cherries, were also grown. The villa had been sited within two miles of the Fosse Way, and produce of the farm was not only sent to market in nearby Corinium (Cirencester), but had easy access along the fine Roman road network to the rest of Britain.

It was not until the early fourth century that the villa was converted into a luxury home. A garden courtyard was built in the centre of the site, surrounded by verandas with additional rooms off them, which linked the three previously separate blocks into one. The dining room was greatly enlarged, new Turkish-style steam baths were installed and the original baths converted into a sauna. The water supply was enhanced by a new reservoir, which now also fed a shrine to a water goddess. Later still, around 370 AD, eight elaborate mosaic floors were laid.

It is unlikely that the initial villa was built by a 'Roman' i.e. an inhabitant of Rome. It is most likely built by a native Briton, probably one of the social élite of the original Dobunni inhabitants, who saw his wealth increasing by espousing Roman agricultural methods. Who owned the villa in its later years is unknown, but it seems likely that its owners were no longer primarily engaged with running a working farm, but were possibly employed in the administration of the country, working in nearby Corinium (Cirencester) but with a family home within easy commuting distance.

Chedworth villa is open to the public 1 March–30 November, 10am–5pm (closed Mondays); February, Tuesday–Friday, 10am–4pm. There is an admission charge, free to National Trust members.

- After viewing the villa, continue up the footpath to the left of the museum and entrance building.

- Soon pass under a railway bridge and continue up the steep stony path.

- 250 yards past the bridge, at a cross track, turn left. Follow the track through trees for a quarter of a mile to reach a stile at the edge of the woods.

- Cross the stile and keep ahead up the field, aiming just to the right of a fence seen ahead.

- Keep ahead, the fence on your left hand, to reach gates in the corner of the field.

- Keep ahead through the gate in front of you and go along an enclosed footpath, ignoring a gate and path to your left.

- Ignore a stile on your left but go forward, going steeply down wooden steps to reach a stile.

- Cross the stile and keep ahead down the left side of the field.

- On reaching a house on your right, turn right over a stile beside a gate, to the right of the house.

- Continue ahead along a lane between houses, towards the church seen ahead.

St Andrew's Church started as a simple Norman building, but was greatly enriched by money earned in the woollen trade in the 15th century. Dates carved on the nave walls are in Arabic numerals, at a time when Roman numerals were still the norm, an indication of the international influences brought back to the Cotswolds by the wool trade. On one of the corbels in the nave roof is a carved head of Elizabeth of York, wife to Henry VII, who visited Chedworth in 1491. In the village, Queen Street is another reminder of this visit.

- Just after passing the church on your right hand, bear left down a footpath at the end of a row of cottages. Follow the footpath back to the Seven Tuns.

Walk 5

Offa's Dyke: the western frontier of Saxon England

Distance: 4 miles

Map: OS 162

Start and parking: The walk starts from the Old Railway station in Tintern Parva (grid ref: 538007). Tintern Parva is on the A466, six miles north of Chepstow and eight miles south of Monmouth. (It is actually in Wales, there being no suitable parking spot in Gloucestershire!) There is a small parking charge.

Refreshments: Café at Old Railway Station, public house at Brockweir.

Historical Background

With the departure of the Roman legions in 410 AD, centralised government soon collapsed, and Britain deteriorated into a host of small kingdoms, often centred upon a town or on tribal lands. This deterioration was hastened by the steady encroachment by warlike Germanic raiders, who came to England initially for plunder but soon settled. Within two centuries Britain was a patchwork of small kingdoms locked in near constant warfare, Angles and Saxons in the south and east, native British, or Celts, in the west and north. Over time the Celts were steadily pushed back into the margins of Britain by their Saxon neighbours, who in turn vied with each other for supremacy. Three kingdoms in particular came to dominate England, Northumberland, Wessex and Mercia. Power shifted between them as first one then another became temporarily supreme.

During the eighth century Mercia, centred on the Midlands, rose to pre-eminence and its King, Offa, became the first man since Roman times who could with any justice claim to rule all of England. Offa came to power in 757 AD, and set about restoring Mercia's fortunes, which had declined during the civil war that had followed the murder of his predecessor. Firstly Wessex was pushed out of Mercia, and the kingdom of the Hwicce, centred upon Gloucester, was seized. Next Sussex, then Wessex, then Kent, then East Anglia were all subjugated in war, and Northumbria turned into an effective client state by a marriage alliance. In 794 Offa was able to claim the title of 'Bretwalda', or ruler, over all the Saxons south of the Humber.

Offa was a strong and ruthless soldier, but also a statesman of great stature. He stabilised England's currency with the introduction of the silver penny, concluded successful trade agreements abroad which greatly enhanced the economy, and was the only monarch in western Europe to be treated as an equal by the great Frankish king, Charlemagne. By his death in 796 AD, Offa had laid the foundations for a stable Saxon state covering all of modern England, and had formalised the frontier with the Celts of Wales by building what is the most lasting memory of his reign, the earthworks known as Offa's Dyke.

The Walk

This walk climbs steadily through woods to a ridge above the Wye valley, and then follows Offa's Dyke for over a mile to the Devil's Pulpit, with views down over Tintern Abbey. It then returns through woods and along the banks of the Wye.

For centuries the valley of the River Wye was a major artery of trade, with wood and charcoal being transported to the glass kilns of Bristol, oak bark to the tanning businesses of Chepstow, and iron from the western Forest of Dean to the rest of England. Freight could only be moved slowly, by horseback up along the valley or by barge along the river, and local industries faced increasing competition from less remote areas.

In 1876 the Wye Valley Railway was built in the hope of reversing this economic decline. The line ran for 13 miles from Monmouth to Chepstow, following the valley floor and necessitating the building of two tunnels, at Tiddenham and at Tintern. There were four stations and six halts along the railway, which was single track for its entire route apart from here at Tintern, where a short stretch of double track allowed trains to pass each other. The line did not prove to be particularly economic, and also had the unforeseen effect of introducing outside competition into the valley, which in turn resulted in the closure of a number of local industries.

The line was closed to passengers in 1959 and for goods in 1964. Tintern Station was reopened as a museum in 1982.

The Wye Valley Railway Museum at Tintern Parva Station is open April–end October. Admission is free.

- From the car park walk past the station buildings and continue along a broad track (the old railway line) past a childrens' play area.

- Continue along the track for quarter of a mile to reach steps leading on to Brockweir bridge. Climb steps and turn right on to the bridge.

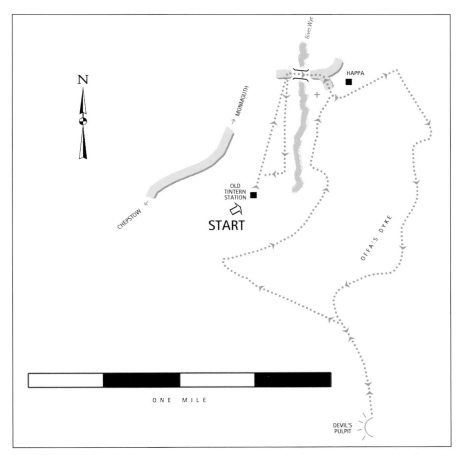

This bridge was built in 1906 by Ironfounders & Co of Chepstow. Prior to this, the only way across the river was by ferry.

● Follow the bridge across the river into Brockweir.

For many centuries the River Wye, along with the Severn, was the major trade route into and out of the Forest of Dean, and Brockweir was once an important river port. The remains of an almost complete wharf can still be seen on the river front. Brockweir was the furthest point up-river that large boats could come. Coal and iron was brought overland to Brockweir, loaded on to boats and sent downstream to Chepstow. The same boats brought back goods to Brockweir for shipment inland, or upstream by barge to Monmouth. The barges were hauled up river by gangs of men harnessed into teams of eight, and at its height in the early 19th century there were 16 public houses in the village to cater for thirsty hauliers. Brockweir was also a boat-building centre. Boats of up to 100 tons built here, and, after improvements to the quays in 1824, up to 500 tons.

Offa's Dyke.

The arrival of the railway in 1876 ended this waterborne trade, and Brockweir's economic significance declined rapidly.

- Walk past Brockweir Country inn and bear right, passing Malthouse on the left-hand corner.

- Follow the road to the entrance to a farm and turn right, signed HAPPA (The Horses and Ponies Protection Association) car park. Walk past the farmhouse and farm entrance on your left.

- In 50 yards turn left, passing buildings on your left and signed 'Offa's Dyke path'.

- Keep ahead up a stony track, past the barns and stables and then the car park of HAPPA.

- Keep ahead, still on the track, up the side of a field, a fence and hedge on your right. The track becomes enclosed and leads to a metal field gate.

- Go through the gate and keep ahead up the field, the hedge still on your right.

- At a finger post, bear quarter right and follow Offa's Dyke Path, now an enclosed, stony, shady track.

- Follow the path to a stile beside a metal gate.

- Go over the stile and turn right for 10 yards, and then go three-quarters left up the slops. A waymark post becomes visible as you ascend.

- At the waymark post turn left in front of the bushes, and then five yards later turn right to go diagonally up the slope.

- At a T-junction at the top of the slope, turn right. Walk with the fence on your left hand and a drop on your right.

The raised embankment you are walking upon is Offa's Dyke, an earthwork raised between 784 and 797 along the whole border between Mercia and Wales.

King Offa had led military expeditions into Wales in 778, 784 and 796. All these expeditions had been aimed to subjugate the Celts, the survivors of Britain's pre-Saxon peoples, and dissuade them from raiding into Mercia. After his 784 AD expedition, Offa conceived the idea of formally marking the frontier of his lands with a continuous earthwork, or dyke. This idea was not new: Offa's predecessor Aethelbald had already built an earthwork across the north Cheshire plain to mark his frontier, and there are numerous other such earthworks across southern England, most notably Grims Ditch in Oxfordshire. What was unusual was the scale of the project, a huge mound up to 20 feet high and 8 feet thick, running for 170 miles from the Severn estuary near Chepstow to the Dee estuary near Prestatyn.

Construction of the dyke was left to local officials, and unsurprisingly it was built with different techniques and to a variable standard along its length. Indeed, in the north it was never completed in some places. The whole Dyke was, however, designed by a single mind, and is one of the greatest engineering achievements of the 'Dark Ages'.

It was never intended that the Dyke should be a defended fortification, such as Hadrian's Wall. Instead it was designed to demark the boundary of Offa's lands, built on an ostentatious scale designed to impress upon the Celts the wealth and power of Mercia.

The next two miles of Offa's Dyke, where it is raised high above the Wye Valley, is the most spectacular part of the dyke, and one of its best-preserved sections.

- Soon cross a stile and continue ahead, following an enclosed path, sometimes on the Dyke itself, sometimes to one side of it.

- Cross a cross track and keep ahead, still following the dyke.

- In 900 yards, ignore a turn downhill to Tintern but keep straight on, signed 'Devil's Pulpit'.

- Half a mile later, do not cross a stile but turn right in front of it and follow the path for 100 yards to the Devil's Pulpit.

Legend has it that the Devil would stand on this rock and scream insults at the monks in Tintern Abbey below.

Tintern Abbey was founded in 1131 by Walter de Clare, and given to the Cistercian order. Although work started on the Abbey at once, shortage of funds limited its development initially, and it was not until the middle of the next century that the Abbey reached anything like its final size and scale. The main feature of the present ruins is the magnificent church, built over the period 1270 and 1325. The church was 228 feet long, lit by huge tracery windows, of which the great east window, 64 feet high, can still be seen. The whole church was a superb example of English gothic style of architecture. The abbey was one of the earlier victims of Henry VIII's policy of Dissolution, and has stood ruined since 1537.

Hailes Abbey (walk 9), although ruined, is the finest example of a Cistercian monastery to be found in Gloucestershire itself.

- Retrace your steps by returning to the stile and then turning left, back along the Offa's Dyke Path for half a mile, to reach a signpost.

- Turn left downhill, signed 'Tintern'.

- Where a track joins from the left, keep straight on.

- On reaching a track, go half-right across the track and then resume your line of advance along the footpath. Follow the path as it descends steeply through woods.

The Tintern railway tunnel was dug through the spur that you are descending, to enable the railway to maintain a flat route down the Wye Valley. There is a second tunnel a few miles further south, at Tiddenham.

- At a T-junction, turn right downhill.

- 200 yards later, at another T-junction, turn left.

- 30 yards later, at a third T-junction, this one with a brick parapet in front of you, turn right, signed 'Brockweir'.

This is the route of an old tramway, one of many built through the Forest of Dean to enable iron and coal to be moved. The tramways were cast-iron rails resting on stone blocks, and followed natural contours around slopes, avoiding tunnels and bridges. Wagons were pulled along these by horses (see also walk 17).

- Follow the broad path as it descends gently.

- Go through a metal gate and continue along an enclosed path for 200 yards, and then look out for a stile on the left.

- Cross the stile and keep ahead to the river bank.

- Turn right and follow the river bank to Brockweir.

- Cross a stile and keep ahead, passing the white Moravian church on you left.

The Moravian church is a free church, named after Moravia, where the church began, but with an informal order of service that follows no particular creed. John Wesley met some Moravians whilst en route to America in 1735, and their simple faith and piety greatly influenced his later concept of 'Methodism' (see also walk 21). In the first part of the 19th century Brockweir was a bustling working port, with 16 public houses but no church. The local doctor, worried about the spiritual health of the village, invited the Moravian minister in Bristol to remedy the situation. The church was built in 1833, financed by voluntary contributions from the villagers, and has survived ever since.

- Follow a concrete path out to the road. Turn left, and then left again to cross Brockweir bridge.

- At the end of the bridge, descend the steps again. You could retrace your steps along the broad path ahead, but for variety, turn left through a gate on to the riverbank.

- Turn right along the bank.

Offa's Dyke can be clearly seen on the skyline ahead. In the eighth century, when it was not so obscured by trees, it would have been even more visible, and an awe-inspiring sight for Celtic tribesmen on the Welsh bank of the Wye.

- Go through a gate on the river bank and turn right up the field boundary. Climb steps to a gate and turn left back to the station.

Walk 6

Deerhurst and the return of Christianity

Distance: 5 miles

Map: OS 150 and 162

Start and parking: This walk starts from Odda's Chapel, in Deerhurst (grid ref: 869299). Deerhurst is approached via the B4213, itself two miles south of Tewkesbury on the A38. There is a car parking area at the chapel, for which there is a small charge.

Refreshments: Public houses en route, one mile into the walk and also at Haws Bridge: shop at Apperley.

Historical Background

Deerhurst church is all that remains of a monastery that in its day was the most powerful in Gloucestershire.

When the Romans departed in 410 AD they left behind a largely Christian country. Over the next two centuries an increasing flood of pagan invaders entered England from Germany, displacing the native British (or 'Celts' as they were increasingly known) and replacing them with Saxon settlers. The Christian church continued to flourish in the Celtic regions of Wales and Ireland, and from there missionaries were sent back to convert the Saxons, and nurture the surviving Christians who had been driven underground by the invaders. At this time Rome itself was under barbarian rule, and the Celtic church developed its doctrines and hierarchy independently.

In 597 AD Pope Gregory sent Augustine to England to convert the heathens. The kingdom of Kent accepted Christianity, and from his base in Canterbury Augustine sent missionaries across the country. In 603 AD Augustine demanded that Welsh bishops attend a meeting with him at Aust, near modern Bristol, where he harangued them on their doctrinal failings and demanded they submit to the teachings of Rome. Not surprisingly, this was rejected, and the two versions of Christianity remained unreconciled until the Synod of Whitby, 40 years later, finally came down in favour of the authority of Rome.

Welsh missionaries had established monasteries in the Saxon kingdom of the

Hwicce (modern Gloucestershire east of the Severn, and parts of Oxfordshire, Worcestershire and Warwickshire) as early as 500 AD, and the whole kingdom was converted to Christianity by Welsh missionaries around 600 AD. Despite the ruling at Whitby, the Hwicce practiced the Celtic form of worship until the middle of the ninth century, and many churchyards are adorned with Celtic, rather than Roman, crosses.

In 800 AD Aethelric, the Christian ruler of the Hwicce, visited Rome as the official representative of King Offa at the coronation of Charlemagne. Aethelric was impressed by the great basilicas he saw in Rome, and on his return bequeathed 30,000 acres of land at Deerhurst for the building of a monastery, which was erected within four years. Deerhurst became the richest and most powerful monastery in the Hwicce, and a last bastion of Celtic Christianity. Although the monastery itself was destroyed, the monastic church survived as one of the finest Saxon churches in England.

The Walk

This walk starts at a Saxon chapel, and follows the River Severn to the place where King Cnut finally gained control of England,

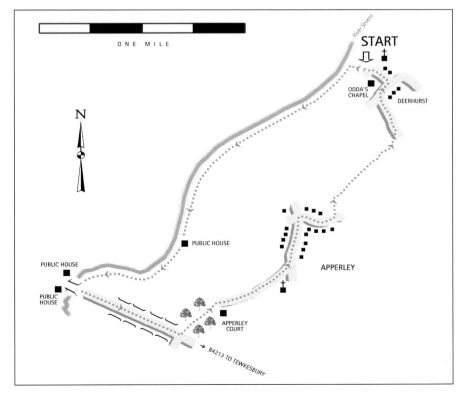

before returning through woods and fields to Deerhurst Saxon church.

● It is worth looking at Odda's Chapel before you commence the walk.

Earl Odda was a cousin and friend of the Saxon king, Edward the Confessor, and in the mid-11th century he was governor of a large part of south-west England, with Winchcombe as his capital. Like his king, he was pious and scholarly, and liked to dress as a monk. In 1053 AD his beloved brother Aelfric died at Deerhurst and Odda three years later erected a chapel, dedicated to the Holy Trinity, in his memory.

The chapel was used as an oratory, or chancel chapel, where prayers for the soul of Aelfric could be sung. It was within yards of Deerhurst Monastery, and was served by the monks there. It was small and simple, but built to last, since unlike most timber-built Saxon buildings it was made of stone. It consisted of a simple nave and chancel, 17 foot high, divided with an arch, and lit by two large windows, on the north and south walls.

Odda died shortly after the chapel was built, and King Edward gave Deerhurst monastery, and Odda's chapel, to the Abbey of Westminster, who held it until the Dissolution in the 16th century. At some stage, exactly when is unknown, a manor house for the Abbot was built adjoining the chapel. The chapel was eventually deconsecrated and incorporated into an extension of the manor. After the Dissolution, the manor, now called Abbot's Court, was sold to a local landowner and converted into a farm, and the very existence of the chapel was forgotten. During restoration work in 1885 the chapel was

Odda's Chapel, now part of Abbots Court.

discovered. Remarkably, the original altar stone, carved with a dedication to the Trinity, was found serving as a window lintel. The chapel, and its altar, was restored, and today stand as one of the very few Saxon chapels to be seen in England.

The chapel can be visited at any reasonable time, admission free.

- From the car park at Odda's Chapel, walk to the end of the tarmacked lane and turn right through a metal gate (marked 'GUAA, Private fishing').

- Go along the track to the river bank and turn left along the river.

- Follow the clear riverside path, keeping the river close on your right and ignoring side turns inland, passing through meadows and past gardens.

- After three-quarters of a mile, pass along an embankment, the river on your right and a lagoon on your left. At a stile after the end of the lagoon, ignore a half-left turn across a field but instead keep ahead, the river close on your right hand. Continue to soon reach the Coalhouse Inn.

The name of the Coalhouse Inn is a recollection of the days when coal from the Forest of Dean was transported by tramway to Lydney, and thence by barge up the Severn to Gloucester and Tewkesbury. This public house came into being to serve the bargees. The opening in 1796 of Coome Canal, from the Severn just south of here to Cheltenham, effectively ended the trade in coal on this stretch of the river.

- Keep ahead across the car park and go through a pedestrian gate, to the left of a gate into a caravan site.

- Follow the footpath to pass between caravans to a stile leading into a meadow.

- Ignore a half-turn left and keep ahead, the river close on your right. Follow the footpath through meadows and over stiles to reach Haws Bridge.

- Cross a stile beside a gate to reach the road.

- If you are in need of refreshments, there are two public houses at the far end of the bridge.

- To continue the walk, turn left along the B4213, looking out for fast-moving cars.

- Follow the road for half a mile.

The flat waterlogged area you are crossing is actually an island, between the main stream of the Severn and a side channel. It was on this island in 1016 that Edmund Ironside, the Saxon warlord who briefly held the throne of England after the death of Aethelred the Unready, signed a peace treaty with Cnut (or Canute), King of the invading Danes. By this treaty England was divided between them, and Edmund agreed to pay a regular tribute to Cnut. Edmund died within weeks of signing this treaty, and Cnut became King of all England.

- Ignore a bridleway that crosses the road and continue along the road for another 200 yards, to reach a lane on the right, to Wainlodes. DO NOT turn into this lane but instead cross the road and take a footpath on the left, leading into woods out of the back of a lay-by.

- Follow the path as it climbs through the wood to reach the lawns of Apperley Court.

- Keep ahead, on a right of way that passes around Apperley Court, the house close on your right hand. Pass through gates to the head of a lane, at a farm.

- Keep ahead along the lane for half a mile to reach Holy Trinity church, on the outskirts of Apperley.

- Continue along the lane, past a war memorial, to a junction of lanes. Keep ahead, ignoring side roads, to reach a crossroads in the middle of the village, the village stores on the left.

- Turn right down Sawpit Lane (signed 'Tewkesbury') and follow the lane for 600 yards to reach the village hall.

- Turn left into the village hall car park and keep ahead across the football field to a footbridge and stile on the far side.

- Cross the stile and turn right, passing a distinctive oak at the corner of the recreation field. Keep ahead across the field to reach a hedge.

- Bear left along the hedge to reach a gateway at a junction of fields.

- Keep ahead in the same general direction, a high hedge on your right.

- At the end of the field keep straight on to reach metal field gates, a redbrick house off to your left.

- Turn left along a sunken lane.

- At a T-junction in 100 yards, turn right along a surfaced lane.

- At the next T-junction, again turn right, passing a telephone box and shortly turning left into a lane, signed 'Odda's Chapel'.

- In 300 yards, pass the entrance to Deerhurst Church.

Deerhurst had been the most powerful monastery in the Hwicce, when that kingdom was incorporated into Mercia. The monastery was destroyed in the late ninth century by the Danes but the church survived, albeit in ruins. It was never fully rebuilt, being by now overshadowed by Gloucester, Tewkesbury and Winchcombe, but in the 10th century the church was reconstructed. The tall nave was restored, round-headed doors and dragon-headed stops incorporated into it, and a polygonal apse, side chapels and a chancel arch added to it. During this period the church remained the centre of a small monastic community. Its most famous member was Alphege, who later became Archbishop of Canterbury and was murdered by the Danes at Greenwich in 1016. Alphege found Deerhurst too lax for his ascetic tastes and left, first to Bath and then to Winchcombe, before going to Canterbury and martyrdom.

After the destruction of the monastery, Deerhurst steadily declined in importance to become an unimportant parish church. Unlike many of its counterparts after the Norman Conquest, it was too insignificant to be either rebuilt or added to, and has not been substantially altered since. Consequently, it is the finest surviving Saxon church in England. Not only are its unique architectural features clearly visible, but it also contains the finest examples of Saxon sculpture still to be seen in situ: there is a Virgin and Child sculpture over the porch dating from the eighth century, and the famous 'Deerhurst Angel' on the east wall is 10th century. The ninth-century font, rescued in 1884 from a local farm where it was being used as a washtub, is the finest Saxon font in existence.

- Continue along the lane to the car parking area at Odda's Chapel.

Walk 7

St Briavels: hunting and ironworking in Norman times

Distance: 5.5 miles

Map: OS 162

Start and parking: The walk starts from castle, in the village of St Briavels (grid ref: 559047). St Briavels is on the B4228, five miles south of Coleford and 10 miles north of Chepstow. There is ample roadside parking around the castle and surrounding green.

Refreshments: Shop and public house in St Briavels.

Historical Background

In Saxon times the land west of the Severn had been part of Herefordshire, and had been designated as a royal hunting forest by King Cnut in 1016. William the Conqueror, like the Romans before him, realised that the Wye was a more defensible frontier against the unruly Welsh, and for administrative convenience he incorporated the Forest of Dean into Gloucestershire. Whilst much of the county was parcelled out between the King's loyal supporters, William retained a quarter of the land for himself. Not only did he own 109 of the 500 manors in the original Saxon county, he also retained the Forest of Dean as a royal forest. There were several reasons for this: strategically, it was sensible to retain the forest in the hands of the Crown as a buffer zone; it was also sensible to retain control over the forest's rich mineral resources, particularly iron ore, rather than letting them fall into private hands; finally, hunting was an important pastime for the Normans, and the Forest of Dean was one of a number retained for the king's exclusive pleasure.

William and his successors formalised the previous Saxon forest laws, making it a capital offence for any commoner to kill any game in the forest. All minerals in the forest were the property of the crown, and could only be mined with royal permission, and even the use of the forest for wood or charcoal was strictly proscribed. However, commoners did have some rights as well as obligations under Norman law, and one group in particular, the 'free miners' of the Forest of Dean, gained and jealously retained privileges for working and living within the forest for many centuries (see also walks 17 and 18).

The management of the Royal Forest, and the protection of its resources from poachers, was placed in the hands of a constable. Initially it was administered from the comparative comfort of one of the nearby royal castles, Gloucester or Sharpness, but by the early 12th century the need for a permanent headquarters within the forest itself could no longer be ignored, and a castle was built for that purpose at St Briavels.

The Walk

This walk starts at St Briavels' Castle and then descends into the Wye valley. It then follows the River Wye for nearly two miles before returning through woods. It is strenuous in places, but offers spectacular views for most of its length.

● Start the walk at the gatehouse to St Briavels' Castle.

St Briavels' Castle was built in 1131 by Miles Fitzwalter, Earl of Hereford, who had been appointed as constable of the royal Forest of Dean by Henry I. The castle was always small, being little more than a fortified keep and surrounding curtain wall. It was not the 'motte and bailey' traditionally associated with Norman military architecture, in that the keep

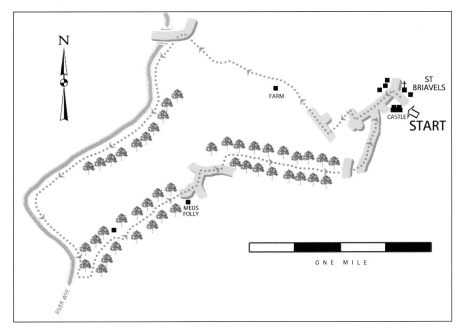

St Briavels' Castle.

was not built upon an artificial mound. Instead it was founded in the solid rock that provides its dominating hilltop position. A well provided a safe source of clean water.

The castle was not intended to be in the front line defending the Welsh border, a function left to the massive castles of Chepstow to the south and Monmouth to the north. Instead it was built to provide a fortified administrative centre from which to govern the forest, a mixture of stronghold, court and prison. It housed the clerks who administered the forest and a small garrison sufficient to enforce the constable's rule, as well as being the home for the constable and his family. The castle was enlarged in the 13th century by King John, to serve as a hunting lodge during his periodic visits to the forest.

As well as managing the 'vert (vegetation) and venison' of the forest, in other words the forests' growing resources, St Briavels' was also the administrative centre for the local iron industry. In Norman England the Forest of Dean was the major supplier of iron, which was not only sold to private industry but was, more importantly, the major source of supply for the Norman war machine. Most of the crossbow bolts, or quarrels, used by King John's army were made in the Forest, and in 1233 his son Henry III ordered 6,000 quarrels to be made, to supply his army in the forthcoming war against France.

Today the castle is used as a youth hostel. The bailey is open to the public April–September, 2pm–4pm.

- With your back to the castle gatehouse, turn left. Ignore a road on the right beside the church but take the next road on the right a few yards later (Cinder Hill, signed 'Lower Meend').

The church of St Briavels was built early in the Norman era, concurrently with the castle, and enlarged in the 12th and 13th centuries. Despite being remodelled in Victorian times, when the chancel was rebuilt and the original Norman tower was replaced, it still contains some fine examples of Norman and Early English architecture, including a Norman font.

St Briavels was a fifth century Welsh bishop, whose name can be found, in various spellings, throughout Wales and Cornwall, and also in Brittany, but nowhere else in the British Isles.

- Follow the road downhill and in 100 yards fork right, still signed 'Lower Meend'.

- At a road junction in 300 yards, turn left and follow the road around a sharp right-hand bend (ignoring two side roads on the junction to the left).

- Immediately around the bend, turn sharp left, back on yourself, down a footpath.

- Follow the footpath steeply downhill. At a building on the left, turn right and in a few yards turn left again, down steps.

- Follow the footpath downhill to emerge in a narrow lane beside Cherry Tree Cottage.

- Turn right and follow the lane. At a fork in 100 yards bear left and continue downhill, past Elmdale Cottage on your left.

- At the bottom of the lane, before reaching the gates of a water treatment plant, bear left and cross a stile by a gate.

- Go forward into a field and turn right. Walk down the field, keeping the hedge close on your right hand.

- In the bottom corner of the field cross a stile and keep ahead along a track.

- Follow the track past a farm and continue for three-quarters of a mile to reach a road.

The lodge-like building on your right, just as you reach the road, was a former toll-house. The poor state of most roads in the 18th century was a major obstacle to the expansion of trade. One answer to this was the construction of privately-funded roads, on which all traffic was charged a toll, in order to recoup the financiers investment. In 1826 the main road connecting the Forest of Dean to the west bank of the Wye was upgraded and the bridge here at Bigsweir built with private money as a toll bridge.

- Turn left along the road for 10 yards. Just before the bridge, turn left down steps and over a stile on to the banks of the River Wye.

- Follow the path along the riverbank for 700 yards, crossing a tributary via a bridge, to cross a stile leading on to a track.

- Turn right along the track. Ignore a gate to the left in five yards but keep along the track, the Wye close on your right.

- Follow the track for nearly half a mile. Just as the track starts to climb slightly towards gateposts, bear right on to a waymarked footpath, staying to the riverbank.

- At the end of the path cross a stile and keep ahead on a footpath along an open meadow.

- Continue along the riverbank for nearly three-quarters of a mile, until woods on the left meet the riverbank again.

- Continue ahead, the river on your right and trees close on your left, for 80 yards, to pass through a wooden gate.

- Continue for another 150 yards to pass through a metal gate into a meadow. Immediately through the gate go half-left up the field to a stile, 10 yards up the slope.

- Cross the stile and climb up the slope into trees (carpeted with bluebells in season) and follow the narrow footpath as it winds along the slope and up through the trees.

- After climbing steadily for 600 yards the path reaches a building. Turn right in front of the building and up a grassy track.

- After 20 yards, turn left up a footpath that climbs into woods, soon with a wall on the left.

- Turn left with the wall and follow it for 150 yards along the side of the slope, before the wall and path turn right again.

- Follow the footpath as it twists uphill, keeping the wall close on your left hand. The path eventually becomes enclosed and climbs to reach a T-junction with a track.

- Turn left up the track, ignoring side turns, to emerge on a surfaced drive at the gate to Meg's Folly.

- Continue up the drive. At a turn in 50 yards, where the footpath goes right, turn left and continue along the tarmacced drive to reach a lane.

- Turn left down the lane, soon passing the entrance to Sitting Pretty, to reach a T-junction.

- Turn right and go along the lane for 150 yards. Just before a house, turn left into a footpath at a fingerpost.

- Descend the footpath. At a T-junction of paths, turn right and go along the slope, a drop to your left. Five yards later, ignore a left turn (signed Offa's Dyke Path), but continue ahead along the slope.

- The narrow path continues along the slope, a steep drop on the left. This path is perfectly safe, but care should be taken in wet weather.

- At a fork after the drop have levelled out somewhat, stay to the right hand, upper, path, and continue ahead.

- Maintain your line of advance along the slope, ignoring any side turns. Eventually a wall is intermittently joined on the right. Continue ahead, ignoring all turns, to join a stream on your left.

- Turn left over a footbridge and climb steps to reach a track. Turn left for five yards to a road.

- Turn left down the road for five yards and then turn right up steps at a footpath sign. Climb a short but steep path up through trees, and up steps to reach the road opposite Greenacres.

- Turn left along the road for 700 yards, views over the Wye valley on your left, to reach a T-junction.

- Turn right uphill back to the castle at St Briavels.

Walk 8

Horton Court: fortified manor houses in Norman times

Distance: 4.5 miles

Map: OS 172

Start and parking: The walk starts at the telephone box in the main (and only) street of the village of Horton (grid ref: 760844). Horton is on a minor road, one mile west of the A46, leading to Wickwar and Yate. Horton is three miles north-east of Yate-Chipping Sodbury, and five miles north of junction 18 of the M4. There is plentiful roadside parking in the village.

Refreshments: None

Historical Background

The Norman Conquest did not see a mass influx of foreign settlers into England. William the Conqueror arrived in 1066 with an army of only 6,000 men, many of them mercenaries who had been dismissed by 1070. The conquest was essentially the exchange of one aristocracy for a different one. William had won a personal kingdom for himself and held on to it by rewarding his followers with the lands of the defeated Saxon nobility. The King granted estates to his barons and to the clergy in return for rent and service, and these in turn granted parts of their estates to lesser landowners. Thus were created tiers of new Norman landowners, who all now had a stake in controlling and protecting the country their King had seized. In Gloucestershire, a quarter of the land was retained as the property of the Crown, and a further quarter given to the Church, who in turn distributed estates to local clergy and lay-tenants.

By the time the *Domesday Book* was compiled in 1086, there were some 40,000 people living in Gloucestershire, in 363 individual settlements. The east of the county was affluent and prosperous, but the west, from the Cotswolds ridge down through the densely wooded valleys on to the Severn plain, was still wilder country, more lawless and with threats of piracy up the Bristol Channel and local banditry. Most communities were small isolated villages, separated from one another by wide tracts of open moorland or woodland. The local lord was responsible for enforcing the law and administering justice, and for the protection of his tenants. He also had to look to his own resources to protect his property and his family. Consequently, the local lords built strong fortified manor houses as defensive homes, no defence against determined foreign invasion but more than capable of withstanding attack from pirates or outlaws. One of the finest examples in Gloucestershire is Horton Court.

The manor of Horton was part of the quarter of the county given to the church, whose tenant-in-chief in Gloucestershire was the Bishop of Bath & Wells. The manor house at Horton was originally built to be the fortified home of the local lord, a tenant of the Bishop and to whom had been delegated the responsibility for controlling that part of the county.

The Walk

This easy walk starts in the village of Horton and goes through gently rolling countryside, past the medieval manor of Little Sodbury and the nearby Iron Age fort, and returns past Horton Court.

- From the telephone box walk uphill. When the pavement gives out, continue uphill.
- At the top of the hill, turn right at a footpath sign (signed 'Little Sodbury').
- Go along the track for 10 yards, and then bear left through the fence and along an enclosed footpath to a stile.
- Cross the stile and keep straight on across a large field (at the time of writing, a permanent-looking 'temporary' fence was on the left hand, marking the route).
- Follow the faint footpath across the field to a stile.
- Cross the stile and descend steeply through a gateway in the bottom of the field, then climb again to a stile beside a gate.
- Go over the stile and keep straight on along the side of a field, a hedge on your right, to a stile in the far corner.
- Continue along the next field, the hedge still on you right, to a stile in the corner of the field, just in front of a house.
- Turn left over the stile and follow a path along the side of the house to a lane.
- Turn right along the lane for 75 yards, and then turn left into another lane, signed 'Old Sodbury'.
- Pass the church on your left, Church Farm on your right, and continue along the lane.

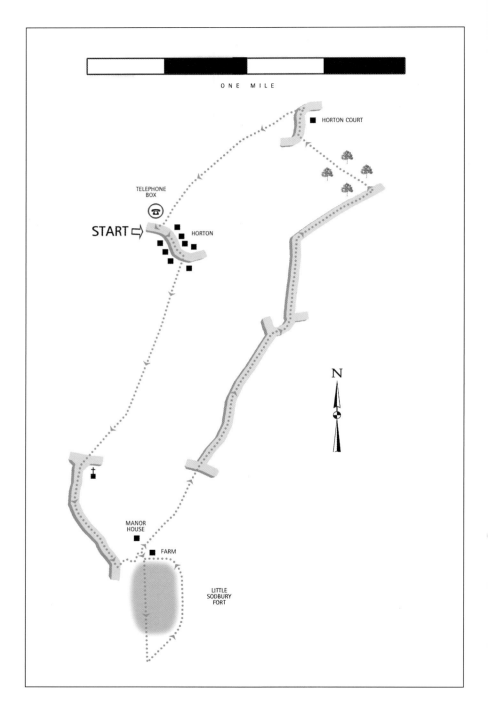

ONE MILE

HORTON COURT

TELEPHONE
BOX

START ➪   HORTON

N

†

MANOR
HOUSE

FARM

LITTLE
SODBURY
FORT

The humps and bumps in the fields on your right are pillow mounds, a hand-built rabbit warren constructed in the 15th century to provide meat for nearby Little Sodbury Manor. The rabbit was introduced into England by the Normans as a source both of game and hunting, and throughout the Middle Ages they were carefully nurtured and maintained, much as game birds were later to be.

- Ignore a footpath going off to the right but continue along the lane, climbing a hill to a T-junction.

- Turn left through a gate and continue up the drive for 10 yards, then turn right up a stony, enclosed footpath. Hidden in the woods up the drive to your left is Little Sodbury Manor.

The manor at Little Sodbury was built in 1486 for Sir John Welsh. Over the centuries it has been added to and converted, and modern farm buildings attached. Although much of the original manor house was destroyed by fire in 1702, the great hall still survives.

William Tyndale was chaplain at Little Sodbury in 1521, his first appointment after graduating from Oxford. He preached widely in the area and first started to translate religious books by Erasmus from Latin into English here. He left the manor in 1523 to go to London embarking on the road that led to his eventual martyrdom (see walk 15).

The manor can be visited by prior appointment with the owner.

- In 20 yards, where the path ceases to be enclosed, turn left up the stony path, ignoring a grassy path ahead.

- Climb steeply uphill to reach the walls of Manor farm, where turn right.

- Follow the path alongside the wall of the manor, and then cross a stile on your left into Little Sodbury Hill fort.

The hill fort at Little Sodbury is one of the finest multivallate (many walled) forts in the Cotswolds (see also Uley Bury walk 2). It consists of 11 acres of flat open land, enclosed originally by a double earthen rampart, with a deep ditch between the ramparts. The inner ramparts themselves are 5ft high above the interior of the fort, and 15 above the outside.

The fort was one of a number of such forts built in the Iron Age. They provided shelter for the inhabitants of the farms dotted around the local countryside in times of emergency, and for the rest of the time to act as an economic and administrative centre for the neighbourhood, in much the way that towns would later do. Regular markets would be held in the fort, secure accommodation provide for long-distance travellers and traders, and periodic courts to settle disputes held here. From coins found at Little Sodbury, it is obvious that the fort continued to function as an economic centre long into the Roman era.

- Follow the path briefly left, and then turn right through the northern gateway of the fort.

Climb the rampart to the right for a view over the fort and over the surrounding countryside.

- Follow the clear path across the centre of the fort and out across the ditch.

The ditch between the ramparts would have been much deeper 2,000 years ago, and the ramparts themselves not only higher but topped with a wooden palisade, providing a formidable obstacle to any potential attackers.

- Follow the faint path to a stile. DO NOT cross the stile but turn sharp left, back upon yourself, and walk along the field edge back towards the fort, the field wall close on your right hand.
- Follow the path between the wall and the hill fort.

As you walk around the ramparts the structure of the Iron Age fortifications can clearly be seen. The inner rampart is very visible; the eroded remains of the outer rampart can be made out, as can the ditch between the two.

You soon pass the main gateway into the fort, leading out to the flat dip slope of the Cotswolds, where most of the farmsteads would have been situated and the major trade routes would have run. The gateway was the most vulnerable part of the hill fort, especially here where it faced flatter land than on the other sides, and consequently was the most elaborately defended area. The complex arrangement of ditches and ramparts around the main gate can clearly be seen. Unusually, the protective ditch is crossed by two earthen entrance causeways. It is probable that the second causeway was put in later in the fort's history, during the settled Roman era, when access for trade was more important than defence.

- Follow the ramparts around, passing the farm on your right, to return to the stile by which you entered the hill fort.
- Cross the stile and return along the top of the bank, the wall of the farm on your right hand.
- At the end of the building, turn right through a gate and then immediately turn left, to walk along the left-hand fence, keeping the fence close on your left and passing outbuildings on your right, to reach a gate in the corner.
- Go through the gate and go half-right across the field.
- On the far side of the field, cross a ladder stile into a lane. Keep straight ahead along the lane opposite, signed 'Horton'.
- On reaching a main road, turn right uphill, signed 'Hawkesbury Upton'.
- In 60 yards, where the main road turns right, bear left along a shady minor road.
- In 400 yards, pass the gates to a large house. 400 yards later, pass the entrance to Top Farm.
- Follow the lane for another 300 yards, and then turn left back into woods, at a footpath sign for 'Horton'.
- Follow the footpath gently down through trees.

- Ignore a flight of steps going up to the right but continue down through trees to cross a stile beside a gate.

- Continue down the broad path across the hillside to a stile in the bottom right-hand corner.

- Cross the stile and turn right along the lane for a 100 yards to reach the gates of Horton Court.

The oldest part of Horton Court, the north wing, dates from around 1140, making it the oldest inhabited building in the Cotswolds. The original house, built of sturdy limestone blocks, was a simple affair. It consisted of a single great hall, which served for the communal living of the servants, a storage area or undercroft beneath, and an upper storey with a chapel and living accommodation for the lord and his family. The Court was built for defence rather than comfort. The original Norman great hall still survives.

In the 16th century Horton Court was the home of William Knight, Bishop of Bath & Wells and secretary to King Henry VIII. In 1527 Henry was growing tired of the failure of his Chancellor Cardinal Wolsey to obtain permission from Pope Clement for the king to divorce Queen Catherine. Henry sent Knight on a secret mission to Rome, with orders were to gain an audience with the Pope. Here Knight was to obtain the Pope's permission for Henry to marry Anne Boleyn regardless of divorcing Catherine, in other words, to get the Pope's permission to commit bigamy. Fortunately Wolsey got wind of the plan, and stopped Knight, to the latter's secret relief. Knight remained in the King's service for several more

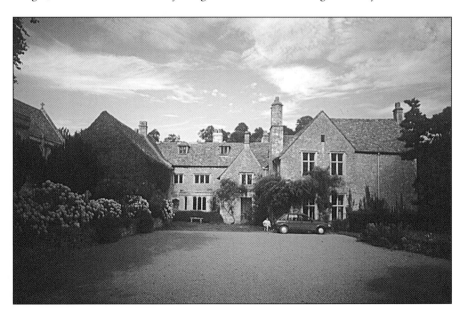

Horton Court.

years, and was involved with a number of further diplomatic initiatives in Rome in the course of the King's 'great matter' (i.e. his divorce).

Knight greatly extended the Norman building of Horton Court in 1521. He later built an unusual ambulatory, or 'loggia', a covered walkway, in the garden of Horton Court decorated with the medallion heads of four Emperors, a style popular in Italy and obviously influenced by his visits to Rome.

Horton Court is open Easter–end of October, Wednesday and Saturday, 2pm–6pm. Admission charge, free to National Trust members

- Continue past the gates of the hall. Five yards later, at a bend in the road, turn left at a bridleway sign, through a gate into a field.

- Keep straight on across the field through a gap in the hedge.

- Maintain your line of advance across the next field, passing to the right of a prominent tree, to reach a gate.

- Maintain your line of advance across the next field to reach a metal pedestrian gate, beside a field gate.

- Go through the gate and immediately turn left. Walk along the side of the field, the hedge close on your left hand, to cross a stile beside a gate.

- Ignore a gateway on the right, but keep ahead for 10 yards to the corner of a hedge.

- Turn right and walk with the hedge initially on your right hand, to a waymarked stile (stay on the level and do not climb the slope).

- Cross the stile and go along an enclosed footpath for 5 yards, and then turn right down a drive back to the telephone box in Horton village street.

Walk 9

Hailes Abbey: the church and the start of the woollen industry

Distance: 5.5 miles

Map: OS 150

Start and parking: This walk starts at Stanway war memorial (grid ref: 061321). The war memorial is on the B4077 10 miles west of Stow-on-the-Wold, and 15 miles east of Tewkesbury, at a crossroads, where a minor road leads north to the village of Stanway. There is ample roadside parking in two lay-bys at the crossroads, in the lane leading south of the war memorial towards Didbrook and Wood Stanway.

Refreshments: Tea room at Hailes Farm Shop, Hailes Abbey.

Historical Background

Wool had been produced in the Cotswolds since the Iron Age, and in Saxon and Norman times many villages were dependant upon sheep for their existence. Scattered communities scratched a subsistence living from the soil and reared a few sheep for meat and for wool. However, the largest flocks were owned by the religious houses. The clergy were the educated class in English society, and there was business acumen in the Abbeys and Monasteries. Much of the soil in the Cotswolds was too thin for agriculture but ideal for sheep grazing, and it was the monks who first saw the potential of using their Cotswolds manors for the commercial production of wool.

The 13th century saw a great expansion in sheep rearing, under the impetus of demand from the thriving cloth industry in Flanders. Much land that had been previously ploughed was turned back to grass and grazed by the hardy Cotswolds sheep. Villages were widely spaced and surrounded by extensive pastures, so this process did not cause the widespread depopulation seen elsewhere in England. It did, however, mean that villagers often now paid their feudal obligations to their landlord by sheering his sheep and cleaning his wool, rather than performing other agricultural duties.

In common with other religious houses in Gloucestershire, the bulk of the wealth of Hailes Abbey came from wool. The abbey owned 13,000 acres of land on the Cotswolds, and grazed huge flocks of Ryland sheep, over 8,000 animals at its peak. The Abbey's wool was exported across Europe, mainly through the nearby port of Bristol. By the mid-16th century Hailes Abbey was one of the richest landowners in the county, and the Abbeys of Hailes, Gloucester and Winchcombe together produced over half the county's wool.

In 1536 the need for a male heir drove Henry VIII to seek to divorce Queen Catherine, leading in turn to his break from the Church of Rome. Church property was confiscated and religious orders dissolved. Hailes Abbey was closed in 1539 and its land sold to local landlords. From then onwards, the woollen industry passed into secular hands.

The Walk

This walk starts at Stanway House, climbing on to the Cotswolds ridge to visit an Iron Age hill fort before returning to Hailes Abbey. It is predominantly across fields and quiet tracks, with a short, steep ascent rewarded by excellent views.

● Cross the road to face the war memorial.

This is quite the most splendid war memorial in the Cotswolds. A bronze statue of St George slaying the dragon, by the sculptor Alexander Fisher, stands on top of an older stone plinth, designed by Sir Philip Stott, who was responsible for the restoration of Stanton village (seen later in the walk).

● Walk down the lane, in the direction of Stanway and Stanton.

● In 150 yards, where the road turns left, just before the gatehouse to Stanway House, turn right down a track, signed 'Cotswolds Way'. Before doing this, you may wish to detour a few yards down the lane to look at Stanway House.

During the Middle Ages the manor of Stanway belonged to Tewkesbury Abbey. The small village was centred upon the manor house and the church, with a handful of cottages clustered around them. The villagers were mostly free men, but with a feudal obligation to work for their landlord, the Abbot, for 15 days a year, sheering his sheep and washing the wool.

After the Dissolution of the Monasteries Sir John Tracey acquired the manor and built Stanway House as his manorial home. The Traceys had been landowners on Gloucestershire since the Norman Conquest, and a member of the family, William de Tracey, was one of the four knights who murdered Thomas à Becket in Canterbury cathedral in 1170. In penance, de Tracey went on a pilgrimage to Jerusalem. To commemorate this he adopted the scallop shell, the badge of the pilgrim, as his personal emblem. The scallop shell motif features prominently on the elaborate gatehouse.

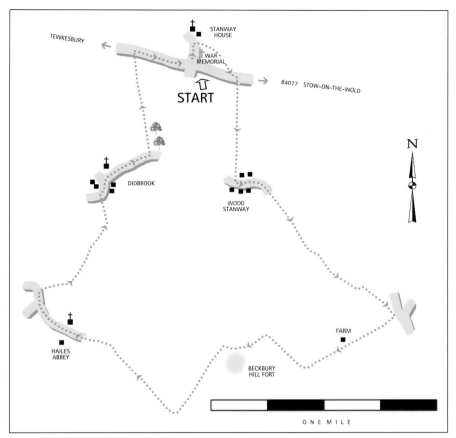

The house is predominantly Elizabethan, with Stuart additions, but unusually is built in an 'S' shape, with the servants and domestic rooms at right angles to the main family range. An enormous tithe barn, a survivor from the days the estates were owned by the Abbey, stands behind the house. The gatehouse was a later Stuart addition, initially ascribed to the pre-eminent architect Inigo Jones, but more likely the work of Timothy Strong, one of Gloucestshire's leading masons.

The author James Barrie was a frequent visitor to Stanway House, and it is said that the image of the sun twinkling off the church weathervane gave him the inspiration for Tinkerbell in Peter Pan. Barrie presented a cricket pavilion, built to his own design, to the village.

Stanway House is open June–August, Tuesdays and Thursdays, 2pm–5pm. There is an admission charge.

● To continue the walk, leave the lane at the 'Cotswolds Way' sign. Pass to the left of a gate leading to a Blacksmiths, and follow the enclosed track to a kissing gate.

- Go through the gate and keep ahead, a wall at first on your right and then with a stream on your left, to reach a stile on to the road.

To your left are the grounds of Stanway House. The Abbot of Tewkesbury had surrounded his manor with a deerpark for his recreation. This was re-developed as a formal landscape in 18th century.

- Turn left along the road for 40 yards, and then turn right into an enclosed footpath (signed 'Cotswolds Way').

- Follow the footpath to a stile into a field. Continue ahead along the side of the field, the hedge on your right, to another stile.

- Continue along the next two fields, keeping the hedge on your right.

- At the end of the third field, go through a gate and follow a short track out to the lane at Wood Stanway.

- Turn left and follow the road through the hamlet of Wood Stanway, ignoring a footpath on your left.

- Follow the lane uphill, passing Whitfield House on your right, to enter Glebe Farm.

The name 'Glebe' indicates that the farm once belonged to the church, and indeed Wood Stanway was part of the estates of Tewkesbury Abbey for 800 years.

- Keep ahead, passing barns on your right. Continue along the track to a metal field gate.

- Cross a stile beside the gate and keep ahead along the broad track up the field ahead. DO NOT follow the track all the way to a gate at the top of the field. Instead, halfway along the field bear left to a stile beside a gate.

- Cross the stile and resume your previous line of advance up the slope, aiming to the left of a telegraph pole on the skyline.

- Follow the telegraph wires through a gate, and then bear half-left towards buildings.

- Cross a stile and immediately turn right up the slope, aiming at a waymark post behind a tree ahead.

- Pass the waymark post and continue to a stile beyond. Cross the stile and go left up the slope, passing another waymark post beneath telegraph wires, to reach a ladder stile.

- Cross the ladder stile and keep ahead, a wall initially on your let. Where the wall bends left, keep ahead on a clear footpath up the slope.

- At the top of the slope keep ahead, following a wall on your right, to reach a road.

There are fine views back across the Vale of Evesham and Bredon Hill.

- Turn right into the road and immediately turn right again through a gate, marked as a Bridleway to Hailes Abbey.

- Go along the track for half a mile, passing barns on your right, to reach a gate in front of a stand of trees.

- DO NOT go through the gate but turn right along the track.

- In 50 yards turn left through a gate and immediately turn right to resume your line of advance along the side of a field, a wall now on your right hand.

- Follow the wall as it bends left around the perimeter of the large field, to reach a gate.

- Continue ahead, a wall on your right, with fine views over Stanway House.

On the left is Beckbury Camp, an Iron Age hill fort. A single rampart enclosed a five-and-a-half acre interior, with a ditch upon three sides and the fourth protested by the scarp slope of the Cotswolds. There was a single entrance on the south-western side. Beckbury Camp is small, and it is unlikely that it was permanently inhabited. It was most likely built to provide emergency shelter for local farmers and their livestock. It is contemporary with Uley Bury (walk 2) and Blackenbury hill fort (walk 15) and predates the Dobunni kingdom that came to rule this area in the 1st century BC (see walk 3). Beckbury has never been excavated, and little more is known about it.

- Pass through a gate and turn right on a path, descending steeply through trees.

To the left is the western rampart of Beckbury Camp, running along the edge of the escarpment and thus providing an excellent defence. Nothing is known about the monument on the top of the ridge, not even the date of its erection. There is a tall niche in its side facing Hailes Abbey, and it is tempting to associate this with a shrine of some sort, but there is no evidence for this. Locally it is known as Cromwell's Seat, reputedly the spot Cromwell sat to watch the destruction of Hailes Abbey, but there is no foundation for this story.

- At a waymark post at the foot of the slope, keep ahead and slightly left, ignoring a turn to the right. Follow the grassy path across a field to a gate.

- Go through the gate and go half-right down the field, to a gate at the end of a line of trees ahead.

The raised strips in the field you are walking through are 'strip lynchets', the remains of medieval field boundaries and terraces. This hillside was part of the estate of Hailes Abbey, and the land here was intensively farmed. The terraces were constructed to facilitate fruit growing.

- Go through the gate and maintain your line of advance down the next field, aiming for a footpath post on the far side.

- Cross the stile and turn right down the track.

This ancient medieval trackway ran between Hailes Abbey and Farmcote just to the south. Farmcote (meaning farm cottages) was the grange farm of the Abbey, and all the land you are walking through belonged to the Abbey. The valley here was intensively farmed for fruit and cereals, both to supply the needs of the monks and also as a cash crop, whilst huge flocks of sheep roamed the hills above, bred primarily for their wool. The stream descending the valley was diverted to provide water for the Abbey and also to feed its artificial fishponds, which provided the only flesh the Cistercian Order were allowed to eat.

- Follow the track for half a mile to reach a lane.

Hailes Fruit farm with its tea room is up the lane to your left.

- Turn right down the lane to reach Hailes Abbey.

Hailes Abbey was founded in 1245 by Richard, Earl of Cornwall and 'King of the Romans' (Richard had been elected Holy Roman Emperor, the only Briton to acquire that title, although it was never ratified and Richard never took up his throne). Three years earlier Richard had survived a shipwreck and sworn that he would found an Abbey in gratitude, and in 1245 his brother, Henry III, gave him the manor of Hailes. The following year 20 monks and 10 lay brothers were sent from the Cistercian abbey of Beaulieu to provide the nucleus of a religious community, and by 1251 the Abbey was sufficiently complete to be dedicated, one of the last Cistercian houses to be founded in England. Richard paid for its building, and gave the manor of Hailes to the Abbey for its upkeep.

    Initially the community struggled financially, but in 1270 Richard's son, Edmund, gave

Hailes Abbey.

the Abbey a phial reputedly containing the blood of Christ, together with a certificate from the Pope guaranteeing its authenticity. A shrine was built behind the altar, which soon became one of the major centres of pilgrimage in England, greatly enhancing the Abbey's revenue. The bulk of the Abbey's wealth, however, came from wool. Hailes was particularly favourably situated to generate first-class wool, and huge flocks of Ryland sheep were grazed on the Abbey lands on the Cotswolds. At their peak over 8,000 sheep grazed on 13,000 acres.

By the time of the Dissolution of the Monastries, Hailes Abbey was one of the 12 richest Cistercian houses in the country. The last Abbot, Stephen Sagar, had Thomas Cromwell as a friend and patron, and the Abbey survived the initial wave of Dissolutions. However, in late 1538 Hailes was investigated, and when its holy relic was declared to be a fake, not blood but merely saffron-coloured honey, its fate was sealed. On Christmas Eve 1539 the Abbey was closed, its Abbot and monks pensioned off, and its treasure impounded. The land was sold to Richard Andrews, a dealer in monastic property, who demolished most of the buildings for their materials, and sold off the land and flocks of sheep to local landowners, primarily Sir John Tracey, who built Stanway House.

Hailes Abbey is open April–September, 10am–6pm; October–March, 10am–4pm. Entry charge, free to members of both English Heritage and the National Trust.

● Walk along the lane, passing Hailes Parish Church on your right.

The medieval village of Hailes was a flourishing community standing astride the Salt Way, along which salt was transported from the salt mines of Droitwich, across the Cotswolds from Hailes to Sudeley, and hence to the Thames and southern England.

The parish church, built in 1130, is all that remains of the village: the rest was completely demolished around 1250 AD so that the Abbey could be built. Its simple exterior, largely unaltered since construction, remains classically Norman, whilst inside the chancel are well-preserved wall paintings dating from around 1300, depicting St Christopher, sporting scenes, fantastic animals and monsters, and the heraldic devices of Richard of Cornwall founder, of Hailes Abbey, and his grandmother, Eleanor of Aquitaine, who was present at the Abbey's dedication.

● At a T-junction, turn right along the road for 200 yards. Here the road bends left, turn right through a gate, at a footpath sign.

● Cross a concreted area and keep ahead along a track, bending first to the right and soon to the left, following the gravelled track and ignoring side turns.

● Where the gravelled track ends, keep ahead upon a grassy track, soon narrowing to a footpath, along the edge of a field, trees and hedge on your left.

● At the end of the field go through a gate and then over a stile beside a second gate. Keep ahead along the side of the field, fence and trees still on your left, for 100 yards.

● After 100 yards, go left through a metal field gate.

- Go along the side of the field, a fence and trees, on your right, to a gate leading out into a lane.

- Turn right and walk through the hamlet of Didbrook, following the road around to the right, signed 'Wood Stanway'. Follow the lane past the church and then the school.

Didbrook church was damaged in 1471, when Lancastrian fugitives from the defeat at Tewkesbury sought shelter in the church, but were finally slain after a brief but bloody skirmish (see walk 14). The church was rebuilt by Abbot Whitchurch of Hailes.

- 300 yards past the school, just before a small wood on the left, turn left at a footpath sign, over a stile.

- Walk along the side of the field, the hedge on your right hand. At the end of the field, cross a footbridge and stile.

- Continue in the same direction along three more fields, the hedge always on your right hand.

- At the end of the fourth field, cross a stile and climb steps on to the road.

- Turn right and walk with care along the B4077. This road is not very busy, but cars move at speed along it. Follow the road for a quarter of a mile, back to the crossroads and war memorial.

Walk 10

Ashleworth: the power of the medieval church

Distance: 6.5 miles

Map: OS 162

Start and parking: This walk starts from Haws Bridge (grid ref: 844279). Haws Bridge is on the B4213, which connects the A38 three miles south of Tewkesbury, and the A417, Gloucester to Ledbury road. Haws Bridge is three miles east of the A38, and is a hamlet at a bridge over the Severn. There is a long lay-by next to the New Inn, which provides ample parking.

Refreshments: Public houses at Haws Bridge, public house at Ashleworth.

Historical Background

After the Norman Conquest, King William rewarded his followers with land taken from the dispossessed Saxon lords. The manor of Ashleworth was given to the Earls of Berkeley as part of their estates. Along with the land, the Earl received rights over the common people who lived on that land, who were required to pay rent to their feudal lord, in goods and in service. Half of the population were 'villeins', or villagers, free men who farmed their own land and had rights to use common land, but who were required to work their lord's land for two days a week, or more at harvest time. A quarter of the population were cottagers, with smaller holdings than villeins, but who still owed their feudal lord service on his land. Both villeins and cottagers also had to pay rent, or 'tithes', sometimes in cash but usually in kind. The rest of the population were serfs, who had no land of their own but worked on their masters land in return for food and shelter.

In 1154 Robert FitzHarding, Earl of Berkeley, gave the manor to the Abbey of Bristol. A quarter of the land in Gloucestershire, over 120 individual manors, was already owned by the Church, and nearly 8,000 people were feudal tenants of the church in one form or another. The Bishop of Worcester, Gloucester Abbey and the Archbishop of Canterbury were three of the county's largest landowners. The Abbey of Bristol was one of the smaller clerical landlords, but the monks of Bristol were far more enterprising landlords than the FitzHardings. They soon developed a flourishing farming business, with the old feudal manor house its centre of operations. Lay monks ran the farm, employing local labourers bound by feudal obligations to work the land. Their tithes, in the form of agricultural products, were collected with ruthless efficiency.

In 1460 Abbot Newberry tore down the old manor house and built a far grander one, to act exclusively as his summer residence. It still stands today. At the same time he built Ashleworth Court to take over the role of the centre of the farming activities. He also built a huge barn attached to the court, to house the produce collected in tithes.

The Walk

The outward leg of this fairly long but easy walk follows the River Severn to Ashleworth and passes the splendid medieval tithe barn there. It returns across fields, a very pleasant walk which requires a little care in navigation in some parts.

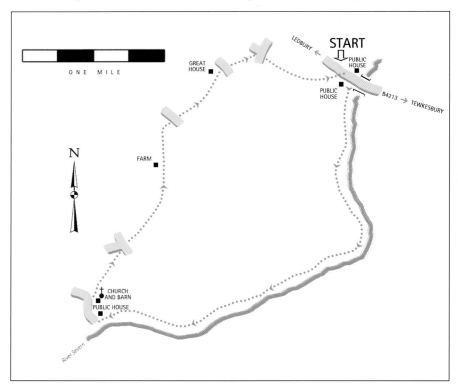

- From the lay-by beside the New Inn, cross the road and go down the access road to the Haw Bridge Inn.
- Walk past the front of the inn and go through a metal gate on to a grassy track along the side of the river.
- Cross a stile and continue along the track, past a house.
- Continue along the track, over a second stile, then over a sluice gate and a third stile.
- Follow the track through two very large fields, the river off to your left all the way.
- In the third field, the path rejoins the riverbank and curves right, cliffs on the opposite bank.
- At the end of the fourth field, continue through a gate along the riverside path, now more overgrown.
- Follow the path through four more fields, over a second sluice gate, and then keep ahead along the riverbank.
- Follow the riverside path through another three fields to reach The Boat public house at Ashleworth.

Until about 100 BC, the Severn valley was thickly forested. The forest around Ashleworth was prone to flooding, and the river itself a major barrier to communication. Where Ashleworth stands, on the west bank of the Severn, the river was fordable for much of the year. In consequence, a settlement grew up here in the Iron Age, and continued to flourish throughout the Roman and Saxon eras. It was only settled by one extended family, which scratched out a subsistence living based upon fishing and harvesting the fruits of the forest.

By Saxon times (500 AD onwards), the Severn valley was largely cleared of forest and provided rich farmland. The modern name comes from the later Saxon settlement, when it was called Aescelsworde, or 'Aescels enclosure'.

- Pass the pub and turn right along the lane, away from the river, soon passing Ashleworth Court and tithe barn.

Ashleworth Court was built in 1460. It is built of blue lias stone, and was originally thatched. It is still an extremely complete medieval manor house, little altered over the centuries and with an intact Great Hall. The court was built by Abbot Newland at the same time as he had the Manor House, half a mile away, redeveloped as a luxurious summer residence. The court was built to take over as a centre for the farming activities of the estate.

The barn was built next to the court and its farm, in 1481, also by Abbot Newland. It is 126 feet long, built of limestone with a stone tile roof supported by oak beams. It has 10 bays inside and two exterior wagon porches. The barn was used to store both the produce of the farm, and also the rent collected in kind from the Abbot's tenants. Nearly a hundred tons of grain, mainly wheat and oats but also rye, passed through this barn each year. Several tons of cheese and butter, and many gallons of honey, were stored, and so too was

Medieval tithe barn, Ashleworth.

wool, produced by the Abbot's flocks in the Cotswolds and collected in Ashleworth amongst other Abbey farms. Virtually all the goods stored here were shipped down river to Gloucester or Bristol to be sold at market, the cash proceeds going back to the Abbey.

Ashleworth Barn is owned by the National Trust and is part of the working farm. It is open to the public March–October, 9am–6pm. There is a charge (by honesty box) for viewing the barn.

Behind the barn and court is the church of St Andrew & St Bartholomew. Originally Saxon, with part of the Saxon masonry still visible in the north wall, the church was extensively rebuilt in the latter part of the 12th century, when the manor passed into the hands of the Abbey of Bristol. The doorway and chancel date from the 12th century, with the tower added in the 14th century and the south aisle and east window being 15th century additions.

- Immediately past the barn and manor, where the lane bends left, keep ahead on a signed footpath, the graveyard wall close on your left hand.

- Follow the field boundary, a line of poplars on your left hand. Ignore a stile on your left, but bend right and then left along the field boundary.

- Follow the field boundary as it bends back left and then right, to soon reach a stile in the field corner.

- Cross the stile and keep straight on across the next small field to a gate into a lane.

- Turn right for 10 yards to a T-junction. Go half-left across the road, to cross a stile in the hedge, at a signpost.

- Keep straight on across the field to a stile, just to the left of a pylon.

- Cross the stile and maintain your line of advance across the next field (second since the lane) to a stile on the far side.

- Continue the same line of advance across the next (third) field, to a stile and footbridge.

- Cross a further stile and go across the fourth field, aiming just to the left of trees visible on the opposite side.

- Cross a stiled footbridge, obscured in the hedgerow at the time of writing, and then go half-left, to go diagonally up the fifth field to a stile in the top corner.

- Cross the stile and keep ahead along the edge of a sixth field, a hedge close on your right, to a kissing gate in the far right corner, next to farm buildings.

- Keep ahead, passing a cowshed on your left. Cross a farm drive to a stile into the field opposite.

- Maintain your line of advance along the field boundary, keeping the hedge close on your left, to a stile in the far left corner.

- Cross the stile and turn right for 10 yards to a metal field gate.

- Go through the gate and keep straight on along the track, a hedge on your right, curving right to reach a gate on to a lane.

- Cross the lane to go through a gate beside a signpost opposite.

- Keep more or less ahead to a stile opposite, in the corner of the small field.

- Go over the stile and maintain your line of advance across the next field (second since the lane) to a stile.

- Keep straight on across the third field to a metal field gate, in direct line with a large half-timbered house (called Great House) seen ahead.

- Go through the gate and then half-right across the fourth field, aiming just to the right of a box hedge, itself just right of Great House. Soon a gate comes into sight.

- Go through the gate and keep ahead along the next, fifth, field, a hedge close on your right hand and Great House off to your left, to reach a concealed stile in the right-hand corner, leading into a lane.

- Cross the lane to a signposted stile opposite.

- Cross the stile and go half-right across the field to a metal field gate.

- Go through the gate and maintain your line of advance across the next field, aiming for a stile 50 yards to the left of the far right-hand corner.

- Cross the stile and narrow footbridge into a lane and turn right for 20 yards to a T-junction.
- Cross the road and go through a metal gate (signed 'Public Footpath').
- Go along the left-hand edge of the field, a hedge close on your left, to a stile beside a gate.
- Keep ahead across the next field to cross a double fence-stile on the far side.
- Go half-left across the corner of the next field to a fence-stile 40 yards ahead.
- Maintain your line of advance across the next field, aiming for a stile on the far side, at the right-hand end of a line of trees and in front of a yellow traffic sign visible in the road beyond.
- Cross the stile and turn left along the drive for 10 yards to reach a road.
- Turn right along the road for 50 yards, back to the lay-by.

Berkeley Castle and the murder of Edward II 1327

Distance: 6.5 miles

Map: OS 162

Start and parking: The walk starts from Market Place, the central 'square' in Berkeley (grid ref: 685992). Berkeley is five miles west of Dursley on the B4066, and four miles north-west of the M5, junction 14. There are two free public car parks in the centre of Berkeley.

Refreshments: Public houses and shops in Berkeley, public houses in Stone and Ham.

Historical Background

From the moment of his accession in July 1307, the reign of Edward II was beset by troubles, mainly of his own making. Unlike his father Edward I, he was no soldier, and his lacklustre prosecution of the ongoing war against Scotland culminated in disastrous defeat at Bannockburn. He made no secret of his contempt for his powerful barons, upon whose support the crown depended, and wilfully alienated many of them. Worse, Edward, a homosexual, flaunted his lover Piers Gaveston, lavishing him with honours and encouraging his vicious wit at the expense of the nobility. In 1311 a group of barons known as the Ordainers, led by Edward's cousin Thomas Earl of Lancaster, rebelled. Gaveston was executed and the king was effectively forced to place the government into the Ordainers hands.

For the next ten years Edward carefully built support amongst those nobles who objected to the Ordainers. In 1321 a revolt erupted in the Welsh Marches led by Roger de Mortimer against the influence of the king's new favourite, Hugh de Spencer. This gave Edward his chance. He crossed the Severn at Gloucester with an army, defeated Mortimer just north of the Forest of Dean, and then returned to capture Berkeley Castle, which supported the rebels. Finally King Edward had Thomas of Lancaster, his lifelong enemy, executed for treasonably encouraging Mortimer's actions.

In 1327 a new threat to the throne arose, this time led by Edward's wife Isabella, a spirited and proud woman deeply resentful of Edward's lovers and his neglect of her.

Isabella raised an army in her native France, and returned to England with Mortimer, who had fled to Paris and was now her lover. The king was deposed in favour of his 14-year-old son, soon crowned Edward III. The deposed Edward was imprisoned, first in Kenilworth in Warwickshire and later in Berkeley Castle. Edward was, however, seen as a potential focus for rebellion against Isabella and Mortimer, and Mortimer ordered his death. Thomas, 3rd Earl Berkeley, was ordered to leave his castle in the hands of Mortimer's agents, Gurney and Maltravers, and on 21 September 1327 Edward was barbarically murdered.

For three years the young Edward III, quiescently allowed Isabella and Mortimer to rule England, until he felt strong enough to overthrow them. Queen Isabella was imprisoned in Castle Rising, Norfolk, for the rest of her life: Mortimer was hanged, drawn and quartered for the murder of Edward II.

The Walk

This walk, although not short, is all on the flat and is not strenuous. It leaves Berkeley Castle and follows the lovely River Avon to Stone, and then crosses fields to return through Whitcliff Deer Park.

- Standing in Berkeley's Market Place, with your back to the NatWest bank, cross the road and walk along High Street opposite, signed 'St Mary's Church'.

- Continue along High Street for 80 yards and then turn into the second lane on the left, Church Lane, signed 'St Mary's Church' and 'Jenner Museum'.

- Pass the museum on your left.

Edward Jenner was born in 1749 the son of the parson at St Mary's Church, Berkeley. At the age of 14 he was apprenticed to a surgeon in Chipping Sodbury. Seven years later he moved to London and finished his training under the eminent surgeon John Hunter. Two years later he moved back to his birthplace, Berkeley, and lived at the Chantry for the rest of his life.

Jenner had always been interested by smallpox, a disease which killed 20 per cent of the population and which had killed an estimated 60 million people worldwide in the previous century. He was particularly intrigued by the country folklore that held that milkmaids who caught cowpox were immune to the deadly smallpox. Jenner devised an experiment, and in May 1796 he took cowpox infected material from a local milkmaid, Sarah Nelmes, and deliberately infected his gardener's son, James Phipps, with the disease. Once Phipps had recovered from cowpox, Jenner tried without success to infect him with smallpox. The concept of vaccination against disease had been born.

Jenner gathered further evidence and published his findings in 1798. Despite opposition from the medical establishment his ideas soon found widespread acceptance, and

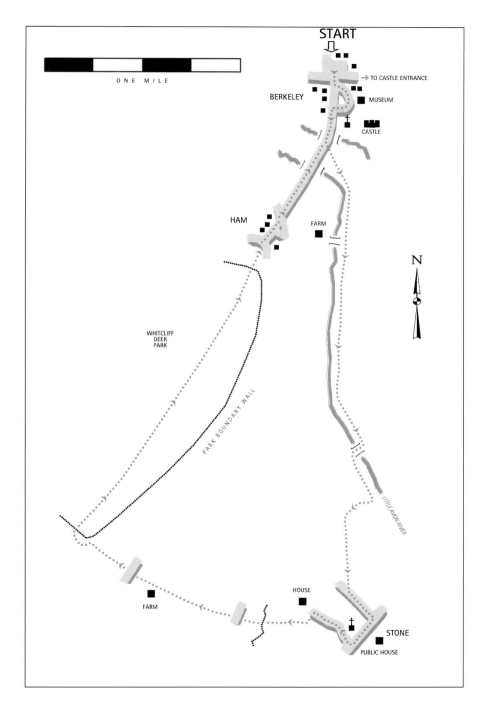

START

TO CASTLE ENTRANCE

BERKELEY

MUSEUM

CASTLE

ONE MILE

HAM

FARM

N

WHITCLIFF
DEER
PARK

PARK BOUNDARY WALL

LITTLE AVON RIVER

HOUSE

FARM

STONE

PUBLIC HOUSE

culminated in a worldwide vaccination programme that in 1980 resulted in the final eradication of the disease.

Jenner built a thatched hut in its garden where he treated the poor for free, and which he named the Temple of Vaccinia. He continued to study in other areas, doing ground-breaking work upon angina and rheumatic heart disease. He also studied hibernation in animals and was one of the first people to come up with evidence that birds migrated.

Museum open April–September, Tuesday–Saturday, 12.30–5.30pm, Sunday, 1pm–5.30pm. Also open Sundays in October. Admission charge.

● Follow the lane to the entrance of the churchyard.

The church of St Mary the Virgin is Norman in origin, and a door survives from that period. It was extensively rebuilt in the 13th century, and contains medieval wall paintings and a fine 15th century rood screen. The separate tower was built in 1753. The church is strongly associated with the lords of adjoining Berkeley Castle, and there are many memorials to members of that family, including the tomb of the 3rd Lord Berkeley, in whose charge was Edward II when he was murdered. The graveyard contains the grave of Edward Jenner.

● Turn right in front of the churchyard gates and follow Church Lane back to the High Street, noting en route the cottage on your right.

This cottage was left to James Phipps by Jenner in recognition of the former's services as a guinea pig in the first smallpox vaccination experiment.

● Turn left down High Street, passing the rear entrance to Berkeley Castle on the left and then crossing a road bridge over the Little Avon river.

● 40 yards past the bridge, turn left over a metal gate, at a footpath signed 'Woodford'.

● Go half-right across the large field, aiming towards a bridge visible at the left end of a stand of trees on the far side of the field.

There are fine views of Berkeley Castle across the field to your left.

The original Saxon manor of Berkeley had been held by Earl Godwin, father of King Harold who was to die at Hastings. After the Norman Conquest, William the Conqueror had given the biggest estates in the more politically sensitive areas of the country to those barons who had accompanied him to England, as a reward but also so that they had a stake in keeping the country subdued. William FitzOsbern, Earl of Hereford was given a manor here as part of western defences, and built a small keep here. The Norman frontier soon moved westwards, into the Welsh Marches, and Berkeley ceased to have much strategic importance.

Roger de Berkeley came to England some time after the initial invasion, less as a military baron than as a courtier who recognised an opportunity for enrichment. He was granted estates of little strategic or political importance, and acquired the estate from FitzOsbern. Berkeley started building the present castle in 1117. It was completed by his son, also Roger, in 1153.

Berkeley Castle.

This Roger opposed Henry II and the castle was taken from him and given to Robert Fitzharding, who was created 1st Baron Berkeley. Despite opposing King John and later joining Simon de Montfort's rebellion against Henry III, the Berkeley family held on to their estates and castle, mainly thanks to Thomas Berkeley, the 3rd Lord, who fought loyally for Edward I in the Scottish wars. It was Thomas who enlarged the 12th century castle into today's magnificent structure. Thomas was appointed gaoler to Edward II and tried to alleviate the king's plight. He was later exonerated of any complicity in the murder of Edward II, which took place at Berkeley in 1327.

Later Berkeleys avoided taking sides in the Wars of the Roses, but used the opportunity afforded by the general unrest to wage a private war with a cousin Lord de Lisle. In 1470 Lord de Lisle was killed at nearby Nibley Green (see walk 15) by William, Lord Berkeley, in the last private battle fought in England. William died childless in 1486, and the castle passed into royal hands until it was restored to the Berkeley family by Queen Mary in 1547.

During the Civil War Berkeley Castle was occupied by both sides, but at the end of the war was not extensively 'slighted' (the deliberate destruction of defences to prevent a fortification being used again). The castle was later modified, with the Norman keep being flattened on the top to give more space. Today the castle is more of a stately home than a military fortress, although the dungeon and cell where Edward II was murdered are still preserved.

For opening times see end of walk.

● Do not cross the bridge, but go over a stile at its end, into the next field.

- Continue forward, the river on your right.

- Follow the river bank for 400 yards, to a bridge leading to a farm. DO NOT turn right across the bridge but go ahead through a pedestrian gate and then a field gate.

- Continue along the river bank for a mile, through water meadows, and passing through and over several gates and stiles, to reach another bridge with a metal gate.

- Cross this bridge and then turn left to resume your former direction, the river now on your left.

- Keep the river close on your left hand to reach a stile in the field corner. Cross the stile and turn right up the field boundary, a hedge close on your right hand.

- Follow the field boundary around a left-hand corner and continue with the hedge on your right, turning back right to reach a waymarked gate.

- Go through the gate and continue ahead, the hedge still on you right.

- Soon the spire of the church in Stone comes into view. Keep ahead through a gate at the end of the field.

- From the gate go half-left across the next field, aiming for the church spire. Go through two gates and out into a lane.

- Turn left along the lane to reach the main A38.

- Turn right and follow the pavement along the A38, passing the Berkeley Arms public house on your left and the church on your right.

- Turn right into a road along the side of the village green.

- Where the road turns left at the end of the green (as Court Meadow) keep straight on along a No Through Road.

- Follow the lane past a farm to the gates of West End House. Immediately before the gates turn left along a bridleway.

- In 20 yards turn right in front of a gate. Continue along the bridleway, initially past the grounds of West End House.

- Follow the bridleway, muddy in the winter, for 300 yards to a footbridge.

- Cross the footbridge and continue, the track now much narrower, for another 150 yards out to a lane.

- Cross half-left over the lane and enter the bridleway opposite. Follow this bridleway for 350 yards to reach a footbridge on your right.

- Cross the footbridge into a field. Go quarter left across the field. Look for a stile, not very visible, halfway along the hedge in front of you.

- Cross the stile and go straight on across the next field to a stile opposite, some 200 yards to the right of the farm.

- Cross this stile and keep straight on, keeping just to the right of telegraph poles, to a stile opposite.

- Cross this third stile and go half-right across a lane to cross a stile beside a field gate.

- Go up the left-hand side of the field to a stile at the top of the field.

- Cross the stile and turn right. Go directly up the bank and through a gap in the undergrowth to reach a red brick wall (the perimeter of Whitcliff Park).

- Follow the wall around a corner, the wall close on your right hand. Go over a stile and continue to follow the wall for 100 yards to a second stile.

- Cross this stile and immediately turn right to go over a ladder stile into Whitcliff Park.

The park was enclosed at the end of the 13th century by the 3rd Earl of Berkeley, and stocked with deer to provide hunting for the earl and his visitors, a major pastime for medieval nobility. The present wall was built between 1770-7.

- With your back to the stile, go straight ahead across the park, following a broad grassy ride, soon through trees along a ridge.

There are extensive views over the Severn estuary to your left, and to the right over the Cotswolds. The Tyndale Monument (walk 15) can clearly be seen on the skyline.

- Follow the ridge through a gate and continue ahead along the right-hand edge of the ridge.

Park Lodge can soon be seen to your right. This crenellated tower is in fact a folly, built in the 19th century at a time when there was a passion amongst the Victorians for romantic ruins strategically placed amidst spectacular scenery.

- Follow the ride for a mile, finally descending a stony track to a metal gate in front of the former gatehouse to the park.

- Turn left in front of the gate and follow the fence for 25 yards, to leave the park over a ladder stile.

- Go straight on across the field, towards the corner of a lane seen ahead.

- Go through a gate into the lane. Keep ahead up the road into Ham, ignoring a left turn towards Clapton.

- Keep straight on along the road, passing the quaintly designed Salutation Inn on your left, and ignoring all side turns. Continue along the lane for half a mile back to Berkeley Market Place.

- To visit the castle, turn right in the Market Place and follow the road leading out of town for 300 yards, to reach the castle entrance on your right.

The castle is open April–May, Tuesday–Sunday, 2pm–5pm; June–September, Tuesday–Saturday, 11am–5pm and Sunday 2pm–5pm; also open Mondays in July and August, 11am–5pm. Admission charge of £5.40 at time of writing.

Walk 12

The Ampneys and the Black Death 1348

Distance: 6 miles

Map: OS 163

Start and parking: This walk starts from a lay-by (actually a loop road) at the village of Ampney Crucis (grid ref: 073017). Ampney Crucis is on the A417, three miles east of Cirencester. The lay-by is a loop road off the A417, at the eastern end of the village. When travelling eastwards along the A417, it is marked as 'Parking', and is also a signposted access road to Ampney Crucis (the second road seen when coming from Cirencester).

Refreshments: Public house at Ampney Crucis: public house and shop just off route, at Poulton; public house just off route in Ampney St Peter.

Historical Background

In 1348-9 the English countryside was devastated by the Black Death. The villages of the Ampneys epitomise the effect of the Black Death upon rural Gloucestershire.

The Black Death was almost certainly bubonic plague, extremely virulent and highly contagious, especially in the crowded and unsanitary conditions prevailing in medieval towns. It caused intense suffering in its victims, with black swellings in the groin and the armpits, the sufferer having a high fever and spitting blood before dying within days. The Black Death had been raging in the Far East for many years, and in 1346 it reached Europe, spreading rapidly westwards. By the summer of 1348 it was in France.

It was believed at that time that the disease was in some way airborne, reportedly spread by a 'thick, stinking mist', and in England it was fervently hoped that the English Channel would keep the plague at bay. In reality, the plague virus was carried by the rat flea, and the rats in turn infested the holds of ships, which continued to cross the Channel without check. In August 1348 a sailor died of the Black Death in Melcombe, Dorset, and within days many of the population of that town fell victim. People fled in terror before the plague, carrying the disease virus with them. The disease was swept across the country by the wave of refugees, reaching Gloucestershire in September.

Due to the nature of the plague it was the most heavily populated areas that suffered the most. Bristol was particularly devastated, but other large towns, notably Gloucester, also suffered badly. In the countryside, the effect was strangely patchy. The Black Death reached the small village of Ampney St Mary in the winter of 1348, probably brought by a travelling tinker, and a third of its inhabitants were struck down within weeks. The village of Ampney Crucis, a mere two miles away, was untouched, despite giving shelter to refugees from its unfortunate neighbour. In Ampney St Peter, only a mile from Ampney St Mary, only a handful of people died. The Black Death reached its peak in August 1349 before gradually dying out, by which time it had killed between a quarter and a third of the population of Gloucestershire.

The Walk

This walk visits the three villages of the Ampneys, passing through pleasant farming land. It uses field paths, well-surfaced bridleways and quiet country lanes, making it an ideal walk for winter months.

- Walk to the far end of the loop road (away from Cirencester) to join the main road.

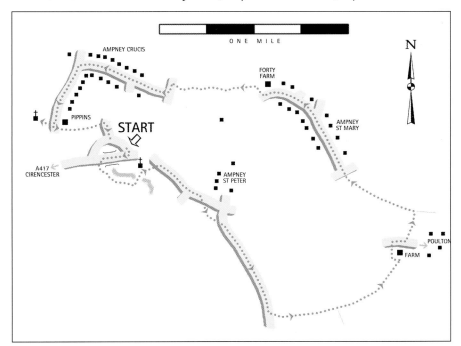

- Turn right along the main road for 50 yards, to cross a bridge over a stream.

- At the far end of the bridge, turn left into a field.

- Turn left again and walk along the bank of the stream, Ampney Brook, to reach a footbridge.

- Cross the footbridge and follow the path through trees to the church of Ampney St Mary.

The little Norman church of Ampney St Mary is all that survives of the original village, which stood upon this spot. Once a flourishing community of several dozen houses stood on the banks of Ampney Brook. When the Black Death struck in 1348 the villagers fled to the neighbouring villages and the church was closed. After the plague had passed, they never returned, instead founding a new village half a mile to the north.

The simple nave is largely 12th century, with a Saxon window and wall paintings depicting St George and the Dragon, and the wounds inflicted by Christ upon those who labour on the Sabbath. There are also some interesting Norman carvings, depicting the triumph of Good (symbolised by a lion) over Evil (two strange, wormlike creatures).

- Go through the churchyard to the road and turn right.

- Walk along the road for quarter of a mile, to pass a lane on the right, to Harnhill and Driffield.

- 150 yards past the lane, look for a footpath sign on the right. Leave the road and go half-right across the field, aiming just to the left of buildings on the opposite side.

The church of Ampney St Mary.

- Walk to the left of the buildings to reach a lane. Ampney St Peter is just up the lane to the left.

Ampney St Peter, settled at the same time as nearby Ampney St Mary, was strangely not affected by the Black Death to anything like the same degree. Many of the inhabitants of Ampney St Mary fled here to escape the plague that raged in their village.

- For the walk itself, turn right along the lane.

- Follow this quiet country lane for three-quarters of a mile, to find a bridleway sign on the left of the lane.

- Turn left into the bridleway and follow the hedge-lined track between fields.

- In quarter of a mile, ignore a bridleway going off to the right but continue ahead along the bridleway you are on.

- Follow the bridleway to a farm. Turn left and then right with the bridleway, to pass around the farm buildings. Follow the farm track out to a road.

- Cross the road and turn right along it for 150 yards, using the footpath.

- Pass the entrance to Ranbury Cottage on the left, and then pass The Old Packhorse House. Immediately past this latter house, turn left over a stile.

- Walk along the side of the house to a second stile, leading into a field.

- Keep ahead, the fence on your left hand. Where the fence ends, keep ahead across the field to a stile and footbridge.

- Cross the footbridge and keep ahead along the field boundary for 100 yards, the hedge close on your left hand.

- In 100 yards, turn left over a stone stile into a green lane.

- Turn left and follow the lane for half a mile, to a road.

- Cross the road and keep ahead along the lane opposite.

- Follow this lane through the village of Ampney St Mary, ignore side roads, right.

The villagers of the original Ampney St Mary fled from their homes when the Black Death arrived, many going to the neighbouring villages of Ampney Crucis or Ampney St Peter. After the plague had departed, they never returned to their homes but instead founded a new village here, half a mile north of the original settlement.

- At the far end of the village, turn sharp left with the lane.

- Pass Forty Farm on your right, and 20 yards past the elaborate gates to Ampney St Mary manor on the left, turn right over a stile and footbridge.

- Go diagonally left across the field to a pedestrian gate in the far corner.

- Go through the gate and turn left, keeping the hedge on your left hand, to reach a stile and footbridge in the field corner.

- Keep ahead across the next field, aiming for houses on the far side.
- Pass to the right of a corner of wall and hedge in front of houses, and keep ahead to a metal field gate.
- Cross a stile beside the gate into a lane, and turn left.
- In 40 yards turn right, along a lane signed 'Ampney Crucis village'.
- Follow the lane through the village, ignoring side turns. Pass Ampney House on your left.
- Follow the lane to a T-junction, at a green triangle, and turn left.

The public house is just up the road to the right.

- Follow the lane for a further quarter of a mile. Opposite a house called Pippins on the left, turn right through a metal pedestrian gate.
- Follow the path across a drive to reach the church.

Ampney Crucis is the largest of the three Ampneys. Like Ampney St Peter, it strangely avoided the worst of the plague that raged in Ampney St Mary's, only half a mile away, and it was to here that most of the inhabitants of that village fled.

The church of Holy Rood (Holy Cross) is Saxon in origin, and in the Domesday Book *the village is called 'Holy Rood Ampney'. Later the name changed to Ampney Crucis ('Ampney of the Cross'). Remains of the Saxon church can still be seen, particularly a doorway in the porch, but most of the building is Norman or later. In the Middle Ages the walls would have been covered with paintings, and some of these still remain in the north transept, including one of only two surviving wall paintings depicting Edward the Confessor. In the churchyard is a fine cross dating from 1415, with detailed carvings upon its four faces.*

- Retrace your steps to the road.
- Turn right for 10 yards. Immediately past the drive to Pippins, turn left at a footpath sign.
- Follow the fence along the edge of the garden of Pippins to a stile.
- Cross a narrow meadow to a second stile, into a sports field.
- Continue ahead along the edge of the sports field, to a stile and footbridge leading into a field.
- Keep straight on across the field, aiming to the left of a house on the far side.
- Go through a gate and keep ahead on an enclosed track, passing the house and outbuildings on your right, to reach a lane.
- Turn right down the lane and follow the lane back to the loop road and your car.

Walk 13

Chipping Campden: the golden days of the Woollen trade

Distance: 5 miles

Map: OS 151

Start and parking: The walk starts from the parish church of Chipping Campden (grid ref: 155394). Chipping Campden is on the B4081, two miles east of the A44 Evesham to Stow road, and five miles west of the A429. The church is on the B4081, at the eastern end of the town. There is plentiful street parking in Chipping Campden, although in the height of summer the town becomes crowded.

Refreshments: Shops, tea rooms and public houses in Chipping Campden.

Historical Background

By the 13th century wool production had ceased to be the preserve of the religious houses, and many secular landowners were giving their estates over to the raising of sheep, 30,000 sacks of wool a year were being exported, mainly to Flanders but also to Italy. Initially the trade was controlled by London merchants, who travelled to Gloucestershire to buy up wool. Local merchants soon realised the advantages of buying local Cotswolds wool and exporting it themselves, usually via nearby Bristol.

During the early decades of the 14th century the demand for wool from Flemish cloth-makers declined, but by then Cotswolds merchants were rich enough and confident enough to begin cloth manufacture on their own account. By 1350 the export of finished cloth exceeded by the export of raw wool, and this trend accelerated over the forthcoming years. The next two centuries were the golden age of wool production. Half of the cloth exported from England came from Gloucestershire and the West Country. The famous English broadcloths were the speciality of the Cotswolds.

Cotswolds wool merchants became very rich men, and invested some of their wealth in building fine houses for themselves and also building magnificent churches for their communities. Chipping ('market') Campden became the regional capital of the wool trade from the 13th to the 16th century. Its weekly market and three annual fairs made it one of the main collection points for wool in the Cotswolds. Many merchants made the town their home. One of the earliest and greatest of these merchants was William Grevel, who not only built a magnificent house for himself but also gave the town one of the finest 'wool' churches in the Cotswolds.

The Walk

This walk starts in the historic market town of Chipping Campden, climbs gently on to the viewpoint of Dover's Hill, and then goes through undulating Cotswolds countryside, crossing fields and woods on well-marked paths.

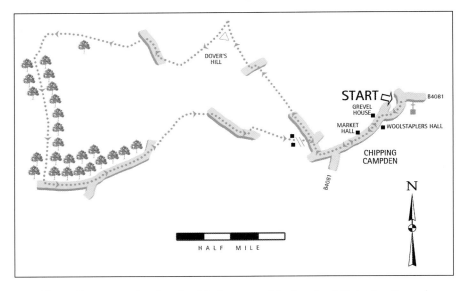

● The walk starts at the church of St James, parish church of Chipping Campden.

St James' Church was extensively enlarged and rebuilt in the middle of the 15th century, a reflection of the wealth of the town. The pinnacled tower was added around 1490, dominating the countryside with its size and splendour. Effigies of many of the town's notable citizens (and the church's major benefactors) can be found in the church, including the merchant William Grevel, and Sir Baptist Hicks, 1st Viscount Campden. There is also the tomb of Thomas, Lord Campden, an important merchant who became first governor of the East India Company. The church contains a fine collection of medieval embroidery.

As the woollen industry took off, and the wealth of the wool towns increased during the 15th century, many Cotswolds churches were enlarged, and a comparatively small team of

Chipping Campden almshouses.

*master builders and masons gained the commissions for the work. The nave in St James'
was built around 1488 by the same master mason that had already rebuilt the church in
nearby Northleach. The pinnacled towers seen on so many of the Cotswolds wool churches
are a characteristic trademark of these jobbing builders.*

*Next to St James' once stood Old Campden House, the greatest mansion in the town,
built in 1613 for Sir Baptist Hicks, first Viscount Campden, the town's leading merchant
and financier at the time. Hicks died in 1629 and the mansion did not long survive him,
being burnt to the ground by Royalists during the Civil War, to prevent it falling into the
hands of advancing parliamentary forces. Today all that survives are the ornate gatehouse,
next to the church, and a stable block, later converted into a Dower House (a home for the
owner's widowed mother), which can be seen in the grounds.*

- With your back to the gatehouse of the demolished Old Campden House, walk
  ahead down the road, soon passing almshouses on your right.

*The almshouses were also built by Sir Baptist Hicks in 1613. Hicks had made his fortune
as a 'middleman' in the cloth trade, not in Chipping Campden (which was already
declining as a wool centre by then) but in the southern Cotswolds and in London. The
almshouses are built in the shape of the letter 'I', in honour of King James I ('Iacobus' being
the latin version of his name).*

- Follow the road around a right-hand bend, past the Eight Bells public house, to a
  T-junction with the main road. Turn left along High Street.

Grevel's House is almost opposite the junction. This magnificent house was built in 1380 by William Grevel, self styled as 'the flower of the wool merchants of all England', whose huge monument can be found in St James's. It was the first of the magnificent merchants' houses that were to grow up along Chipping Campden's main street in the centuries that followed. Grevel died in 1401 and his ornate tomb is in St James's.

- Continue along the High Street, passing Woolstaplers Hall and Bedford House on your left.

Woolstaplers Hall was built around 1400 by Robert Calf, a wool merchant, but soon became the headquarters of the Woolstaplers, the guild of wool merchants that was formed to keep control of the local wool trade in their own hands. After Grevel's House, this is one of the earliest buildings in Chipping Campden. Today the Woolstaplers Hall is a museum to the local wool trade.

Woolstaplers Hall is open Tuesday–Saturday, 10am–5pm, Sunday, 2pm–5pm. There is an admission charge.

By contrast, nearby Bedford House is one of the last of the great houses to be built on the High Street. It was built around 1745 by Thomas Woodward. Chipping Campden's importance as a wool town was well into decline by the mid-18th century, but Woodward had made his fortune as a mason and quarry owner.

- Pass the market hall on your right.

The market hall was built in 1627 by Sir Baptist Hicks, first Viscount Campden, to house the butter, cheese and poultry market held weekly in the town.

The width of Chipping Campden's High Street reveals its origins as a market. It contains magnificent buildings from the 14th century onwards, a mixture of styles and ages. However, they all reflect the towns prosperity as the centre of the Cotswolds wool trade, from the middle ages until the 17th century.

- Continue along the High Street until you reach a catholic church and school on your right. Immediately turn right along a lane, signed 'Cotswolds Way'.

- In 100 yards, where the lane turns right, keep ahead up Hoo Lane.

- Where Littleworth joins from the left, keep ahead, signed 'No Through Road'.

- Where the tarmac ends, keep straight on up the track, signed 'Cotswolds Way'.

- Pass a farm entrance on your left. Keep ahead into an enclosed footpath to the left of the track, farm buildings initially close on your left.

- Continue up the footpath for a quarter of a mile, passing through several squeeze stiles, to reach a lane.

- Turn left along the lane for 80 yards and then turn right into an enclosed footpath, still signed 'Cotswolds Way'.

- Follow the footpath to a stile. Cross the stile into a field and continue ahead with the hedge on your right for 150 yards, until you converge with the scarp slope on your left. Turn sharply left, back on yourself, and walk along the escarpment to the trigulation point (there is no right of way from the stile to the trigulation point, and besides, the short detour along the escarpment edge is worth it for the views).

Dover's Hill is named after a local lawyer, Captain Robert Dover, who in 1612 founded annual local games, nicknamed the Cotswold 'Olympicks', which were held each Whitsun on this spot. The Oylmpicks consisted of cock-fighting, bull-baiting and horse racing, as well as numerous physical games, including wrestling, boxing, and shin-kicking, a 'sport' local to the Cotswolds. The games were very popular but became increasingly marred by drunkenness and violence, and were abolished in 1853. They were revived in 1951 for the Festival of Britain and are still held every May, in a less robust form.

From Dover's Hill there are extensive views across the Vale of Evesham, with the Malvern Hills and Bredon Hill clearly visible, and on clear days even the mountains of South Wales can be seen.

- Continue past the trigulation point along the escarpment to reach a toposcope.

Sheep still graze these slopes, as they have done for a thousand years and upon which the fortunes of the Cotswolds were based.

- Immediately past the toposcope, turn right down a grassy track to a kissing gate on the left, 30 yards uphill from a field gate.

- Go through the kissing gate into a lane and turn right down the lane for 200 yards, then turn left over a stile at a finger post.

- Keep ahead along the bottom of the field, parallel to a hedge on your right, to reach a gate in the bottom right-hand corner of the field.

- Go through the gate and keep straight on down the next field to a stile in the fence at the bottom.

- Cross the double stile and continue straight on, aiming for an isolated clump of trees apparently on the edge of the slope ahead.

- A stile comes into view just after passing over the crest of the field. Cross this stile and continue down the next field, a fence and hedge on your left.

- Cross a drive at a finger post, a 100 yards to the right of a house.

- Continue down the next field, and then veer left to reach the nearest of two stiles in the bottom left-hand corner of the field.

- Cross the stile and walk along the bottom of the field, a fence initially on your right. When the fence turns right, keep straight on across the field, a brook off to your right, to reach a stile in the far right-hand corner of the field.

- Cross the stile and the brook and turn left up a footpath, keeping the brook close on your left hand.

Chipping Campden.

- Follow the footpath uphill, the brook on your left, to reach a gate.

- Go through the gate and keep straight on, a fence and hedge on your left. Follow the footpath into the next field.

- Follow the footpath along the field edge, through trees, crossing the brook and climbing up the field, the hedge still on your left, to reach a stile beside a gate.

- Cross the stile and climb a track, soon passing between gate posts.

- Continue uphill on the track to reach a gate on to a lane.

- Turn left along this quiet tree-lined lane for quarter of mile to reach a main road.

- Keep ahead along the main road for another quarter of a mile. Where the road bends left, look for a 'Cotswolds Way' sign on the right, just past a gate.

- Turn right and then immediately left, to follow a footpath along the field edge, initially parallel to the road on your left.

- After 400 yards, and 100 yards short of the field end, turn right and follow a distinct path across the field, making directly for the tower of Chipping Campden church seen below.

There is a splendid view down into the valley, which is dominated by the pinnacled tower of St James' church, Chipping Campden.

- On reaching a lane, turn right downhill.

This lane is called Dyers Lane, its name a reflection of the woollen industry, which dominated the region in the Middle Ages. Cloth dyers lived along this lane, drawing water from local streams in order to aid the process of dying raw wool.

- In 300 yards, just after the lane has bent left after passing houses, turn left at a footpath sign.

- Cross a stile on your right into a field. Follow a vague path quarter left across the field, bearing away from Dyers Lane and aiming towards the right end of a row of houses on the far side of the field.

- Leave the field at a footpath post, beside a telegraph pole, and go along a short track between houses to a road.

- Cross the road and continue ahead along an enclosed footpath, to reach a second road.

- Turn right back to the main road, and then turn left back into Chipping Campden.

- Retrace your outward steps along the High Street as far as Grevel's House. Instead of turning right back towards the church, you may care to continue along the splendid main road for a further 200 yards. This will bring you to the Ernest Wilson Memorial Garden.

Ernest 'Chinese' Wilson was a local botanist, born in Chipping Campden in 1876, who in 1899 was commissioned by the exotic nursery Veitch & Sons, to journey to China and return with as many exotic plants as he could find. Wilson had numerous adventures, refusing to shed his distinctive European clothing despite travelling in a country in the grips of the Boxer Rebellion (an intensely nationalist uprising against foreign intervention in Chinese affairs, in which westerners were a particular target for the rebels). His major claim to fame was the discovery of Wilsons Chinese Gooseberry, later commercially grown in New Zealand under the name 'kiwi fruit'.

Walk 14

The battle of Tewkesbury 1471

Distance: 3 miles

Map: OS 150

Start and parking: The walk starts from the Market Cross in the centre of Tewkesbury, at the junction of Barton Street, High Street and Church Street (grid ref: 893327). Tewkesbury town centre is compact and the Market Cross is right in the middle of town. There are numerous pay and display car parks in Tewkesbury, and it is recommended that you use the most convenient one and make your way to the start.

Refreshments: Numerous public houses, shops and tea rooms in Tewkesbury.

Historical Background

By the spring of 1471 the 20-year conflict known as the Wars of the Roses was reaching its climax. The previous autumn the Earl of Warwick (the 'Kingmaker') had driven the Yorkist King Edward IV into exile and restored the Lancastrian King Henry VI to his throne. Although Warwick held both King Henry and London town his position was by no means secure, and he repeatedly entreated Henry's queen, the martial Margaret of Anjou, to return from exile in France to aid him. Margaret, who mistrusted Warwick and had no faith in Henry's abilities to rule, delayed.

In April 1471 Edward IV returned to England at the head of an army, and marched upon London. Belatedly, Queen Margaret decided to help Warwick, and with her son Prince Edward, landed at Weymouth at the head of a French army. On the day of her landing, King Edward defeated and killed Warwick at the battle of Barnet. Victorious, he re-imprisoned King Henry and then marched south to deal with Margaret.

Queen Margaret, short on manpower, left Devon and headed towards Lancashire, where she would be able to raise men to her banner. Edward anticipated her plan and marched rapidly westwards from London to intercept her. Edward narrowly missed the Lancastrian army at Bath on 30 April, and pursued them northwards to Bristol. Margaret, anxious to avoid battle until she could gain reinforcements, again slipped away and headed towards Gloucester, hoping to cross the Severn into Wales, friendly to her cause. However, Gloucester was firmly held by troops loyal to Edward and Margaret was forced again to march up the Severn, aiming for the next crossing point, Tewkesbury.

In the late afternoon of 3 May the exhausted Lancastrian army reached Tewkesbury, with Edward only three miles behind them, too close for Margaret to be able to cross the Severn before Edward was upon her. The Queen and her army camped that night just outside the town, knowing that battle could no longer be avoided. On 4 May, in one of the bloodiest battles of the Wars of the Roses, King Edward roundly defeated Queen Margaret's army. Margaret's son Prince Edward died in the battle and in its aftermath, the Lancastrian leaders were executed, and King Henry VI was slain in the Tower of London. Edward IV was secure on his throne for the rest of his reign.

The Walk

This short walk is largely within the town of Tewkesbury and the surrounding meadows, and follows the course of the battle of Tewkesbury on 4 May 1471.

- Opposite the market cross is the Methodist church.

In 1676 three-quarters of the population of Tewkesbury were non-conformist, many of them Baptists, whose chapel is a little further down Church Street. Tewkesbury was fertile ground for the preachings of John Wesley, who travelled extensively throughout Gloucestershire in the 1740s (see walk 21), preaching the message of 'Methodism', which involved strict adherence to religious precepts and putting faith into practice.

- Facing the Market Cross, with your back to the Methodist Church, turn left and walk along Church Street, passing the Royal Hop Pole public house on the right.

- Just before the Abbey, turn left into Gander Lane.

- Follow the lane across the bridge over the River Swilgate, towards the car park.

- Follow the lane down the side of the car park to the end of the lane, at the gates of a caravan park. Bear right through metal gates, the gateposts commemorating the reign of George V.

In 1471 Tewkesbury was a small cluster of houses and inns around the Abbey. To the south of the town, where the battle was fought, was undulating countryside, cut by many hedges, deep ditches, and narrow muddy tracks. There was a narrow road, leading south towards Gloucester, roughly following the same routs as the present A438 Gloucester Road.

- Follow the tarmacked path, passing between a bowling green and a children's play area.

- Follow the path towards houses.

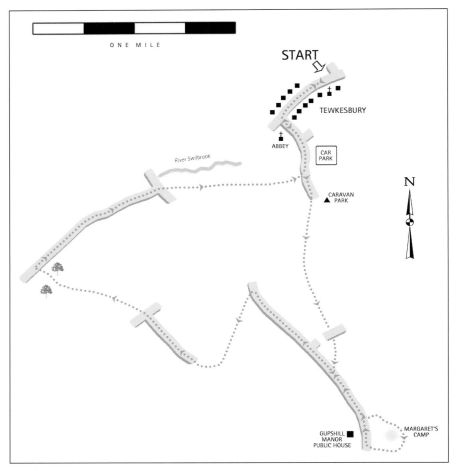

It was traditional for a medieval army to be arranged in three distinct groups of men, or 'battles' (later called 'battalions'). The battles formed a line, one battle on the left wing, one the centre and the third the right wing. Where the path reaches the houses was where the Lancastrian army was drawn up on the morning of 4 May 1471, facing away from you. The left battle, led by the Earl of Devon, stood where the houses now start: to his left, where the present cemetery is, was the centre battle, commanded by Lord Wenlock and Prince Edward, Margaret of Anjou's son: beyond them, the right battle, commanded by the Duke of Somerset. Between each battle were a few artillery pieces, 6,000 men stood on a front barely 1,000 yards long.

- Continue along the path, the backs of houses on your left and the graveyard fence on your right. Follow the path out to a road.

- Cross the road and enter Conigree Lane opposite. Immediately turn right, signed

'Apperley House'. Take the path immediately to the left of the gate, a high hedge on your right.

- Follow the path out to the busy Gloucester Road.

At this point stood the right wing of the Yorkist army, commanded by Lord Hastings, only 400 yards from the Lancastrian left wing. The ground between was broken by a mass of hedge- and ditch-lined fields.

- Turn left and walk along Gloucester Road for 300 yards. 100 yards after a bus shelter, turn left at a footpath post, along an alley leading towards houses.

- At the end of the alley turn left along an enclosed footpath in front of houses.

- At the end of the footpath go through a gate on the right. Maintain your general line of advance around the field, a fence and hedge on your left hand.

The mounds in the field to your right are called 'Margaret's Camp', and are traditionally the location where the exhausted Lancastrian army camped on the night before the battle. In reality, the mounds were not raised as a military earthwork but are the remains of a moated manor house, demolished long before the 1471. It is possible that this was used as an outpost by the Lancastrians. King Edward's army was camped three miles away, at Tredington.

- On the far side of the field leave by a pedestrian gate and turn right along a tarmacced path. Follow the path as it bears right, back to the Gloucester Road.

- Turn right along the road, passing the half-timbered Gupshill Manor public house.

There has been a coaching inn on the site of Gupshill Manor since the mid-15th century. Queen Margaret reputedly stayed here on the night before the battle.

- Retrace your steps to the alleyway you came out of.

You are now at the position of the Yorkist right flank again. The Yorkist centre, commanded by King Edward, was a hundred yards to your left.

- Continue along the Gloucester Road. Cross Abbots Road and continue for another 100 yards, then cross the road to a footpath post, at the far end of a bus stop lay-by.

- Cross the stile beside a gate and go ahead across the field, keeping the hedge on your right hand. Continue to a stile in the far corner.

You are now standing where the Yorkist centre drew up for the battle. King Edward led the centre himself, and his personal standard flew just about where you are now standing. Cannon were placed between the centre and the two flanking battles.

- Cross the stile and keep ahead, passing between a hedge and a barn. Join a drive at house gates and keep ahead to a lane.

In the field opposite you was the left wing of the Yorkist army, led by the King's brother, Richard, Duke of Gloucester (later Richard III). The wooded hill you can see beyond had a far larger stand of trees upon it in 1471, and Richard placed 200 spearmen in the trees

Tewkesbury Abbey.

to guard against a surprise attack on his flank.

This then was the disposition of the two armies on the morning of 4 May 1471. King Edward's army consisted of 5,000 men, a thousand less than his opponents, but better disciplined, more experienced soldiers, better led and with better morale. The larger Lancastrian army was 400 yards away, up the lane to your right.

- Turn right along the lane and follow it to its junction with a road.

You are now standing at the point where the first action of the battle occurred. After an inconclusive artillery duel, The Lancastrian right wing, led by the Duke of Somerset, charged the 400 yards across the meadows in front of you, to attack the Yorkist centre. In doing this, they crossed the front of the Yorkist left wing, and Richard of Gloucester immediately charged their exposed flank, aided by the 200 spearmen he had hidden on the wooded hill. The two armies crashed together where you are standing now, in a seething mêlée of spears and swords. Somerset's force, fighting on two fronts, was overwhelmed.

- Turn right along the road for 40 yards, and then turn left through a kissing gate.

- Keep ahead along the meadow, the hedge close on your right.

In a medieval battle, large-scale loss of life did not occur when two forces were crammed together fighting face-to-face, but when one force lost its nerve and turned to flee, enabling the victors to pursue them and cut at their unprotected backs. This is what happened to Somerset's force, which fled in disorder across this meadow and were cut down. This field has been called Bloody Meadow ever since.

- At the end of the meadow follow a path through bushes to a stile. Cross the stile and bear left through trees to a lane.

- Turn right along the lane.

There was a muddy, rutted lane here at the time of the battle. The survivors of Somerset's force fled to this lane, their starting position at the beginning of the battle, and then turned right, fleeing to the safety of the Lancastrian centre just ahead of them. They were hotly pursued by Richard of Gloucester and his force.

- Follow the lane to the main road.

The Lancastrian centre stood where the lane met the road to Gloucester. They were attacked from the front by King Edward, then disrupted and disconcerted by the panicky survivors of Somerset's wing running into them, and finally attacked on their flank by Richard of Gloucester. Under this assault they broke and ran. Prince Edward was slain during the fighting here.

- Cross the road to a pedestrian gate opposite, leading into a sports field.

- Keep ahead, the River Swilgate close on your left.

In 1471 this whole area was given over to vineyards belonging to the Abbey. The fleeing Lancastrians ran through these vineyards, pursued by the victorious Yorkists. Some tried to hide amongst the vines and were slain: others tried to swim the River Swilgate, deeper and faster then than now, and, encumbered by their armour, many drowned. Some made it to the shelter of Tewkesbury and hid in the town or the Abbey. 2,000 Lancastrians died in the battle, including Prince Edward. Most slain as they fled, either across Bloody Meadow or here in the vineyards.

- Leave the sports field by a kissing gate and turn left along the road.

- Follow the road to a car park on the left. The Abbey is on your left.

Some Lancastrians, including the Duke of Somerset, sought refuge in the Abbey. They remained there for two days whilst King Edward negotiated with the Abbot for them to be handed over, and were then surrendered to the King. The leading Lancastrians, including Somerset, were executed in the square in front of the Abbey.

- To visit the Abbey, cross this car park and enter the Abbey grounds through a gate at the rear of the car park.

Tewkesbury Abbey church was consecrated in 1121, and served both the Benedictine Abbey and the parish of Tewkesbury. The Romanesque west front, nave, tower and arcading are 12th and 13th century, whilst the nave vault and ceilings date from 1340. The heraldic glass is from the same period. There are excellent fan vaulted ceilings in the Perpendicular style in the Despenser and Fitzhamon chapels. The Beaucamp chapel is the culmination of medieval architecture, surpassed only by that knights chapel in St Mary's Warwick.

The Abbey was dissolved in 1539, but the church survived because the townsfolk paid £453 to the King's Commisssioners so that they could keep it as their parish church. William Morris intervened in 1875 to prevent the church's proposed drastic 'restoration' in Victorian times and thus Tewkesbury has survived as one of the largest and finest Norman churches in England.

The tomb of Edward, Prince of Wales, son of Margaret of Anjou and King Henry VI, can be seen in the nave of Tewkesbury Abbey.

- Leave the Abbey by the main door and continue ahead to reach Church Street. Turn right and follow Church Street back to the Market Cross.

Walk 15

William Tyndale and the English Reformation

Distance: 5.5 miles

Map: OS 162

Start and parking: The walk starts from the Civic Centre in Wotton-under-Edge, in the town centre at the junction of Bear Street, High Street and Bradley Street (grid ref: 755934). Wotton is at the junction of the B4060 and the B4058 four miles south of Dursley and 10 miles south-west of Stroud. There is ample parking in Wotton, and a free Civic Centre car park entered from the B4060 Dursley Road.

Refreshments: Shops and public houses in Wotton-under-Edge; pub just off the route halfway around the walk.

Historical Background

One of the leading figures in the early Reformation in England was William Tyndale, whose monument is visited on this walk.

There was undoubted need for reform of the Church at the beginning of the 16th century. As well as a growing complaint at the wealth of the clergy the actual theology of the Catholic Church was also being questioned, in particular the necessity for the hierarchical structure of the Church and legitimacy of the church's claim to have the sole right to interpret the scriptures. A movement began within the Church demanding reform, based upon the work of the Dutch theologian Desiderius Erasmus. His teachings soon spread rapidly, thanks to the newly-invented printing press, which enabled ideas to reach a wider audience than ever before, and formed the intellectual basis for the movement for reform of the church.

Tyndale saw that the external trappings of religion were accepted by the people without any understanding of their meaning, and increasingly the ceremony of the Church was more important than religious teachings. He argued that religious authority was based upon the scriptures themselves, not upon the Church's interpretation of them. Tyndale believed that the only way to bring back a true understanding of religion to the mass of the people was to give them a bible in their own language. This idea horrified the Church authorities, who saw it as undermining their position. In this they were supported by King Henry VIII, a devout Catholic who had earned the title 'Defender of the Faith' for his learned repudiation of Luther's doctrine. Tyndale went into voluntary exile in Germany, and there in 1524 he translated the New Testament into English. This was soon being widely circulated in England, and in 1526 was amongst a number of books publicly burnt in London on the order of King Henry, as being seditious.

Soon, however, political demands were forcing Henry into confrontation with the church, and Tyndale was invited to return to England to work alongside Thomas Cromwell in the reform of the Church. As a condition, Tyndale insisted that Henry promote the English language Bible. This was too radical a step for the king at that time, and Tyndale remained in exile in Holland. In 1536 he was betrayed to the Inquisition and burnt at the stake in Villorde, near Brussels.

In 1539, having finally broken with Rome, Henry published the authorised English-language Bible, closely based upon Tyndale's original translation.

The Walk

This walk starts with a steady ascent on to Wotton Hill, followed by a level leafy walk past an Iron Age hill fort and the Tyndale monument, with its spectacular views. It returns along quiet lanes and bridle paths.

Wotton ('wool town') was part of the estate of the Berkeley family (see walk 11) and was burnt to the ground in the 13th century by mercenaries in the pay of King John. A completely new town was laid out in 1253 by Lady Katherine Berkeley in a formal grid pattern, which is still visible today. The town flourished with the wool trade, and there are many fine 16-18th century houses speaking of the prosperity of this period. The magnificent 15th-century church contains the commemorative brasses of Thomas, 3rd Lord Berkeley, (see walk 11) and his wife Katherine (not the builder of the town). Isaac Pitman taught at Wotton and devised his system of shorthand here.

- With your back to the civic centre, turn left along Bear Street, passing the Shell garage, to reach the main road at the junction of the B4058 and B4060.

- Cross the main road (Gloucester Street) and go up Tabernacle Pitch opposite.

- Turn left in front of a former church, now Wotton Auction Rooms, and continue up the road, passing the graveyard and later houses on your right.

- Continue up the lane past a No Through Road sign. At the last driveway on the right, continue ahead along and enclosed footpath.

- At a T-junction with a road, turn right uphill.

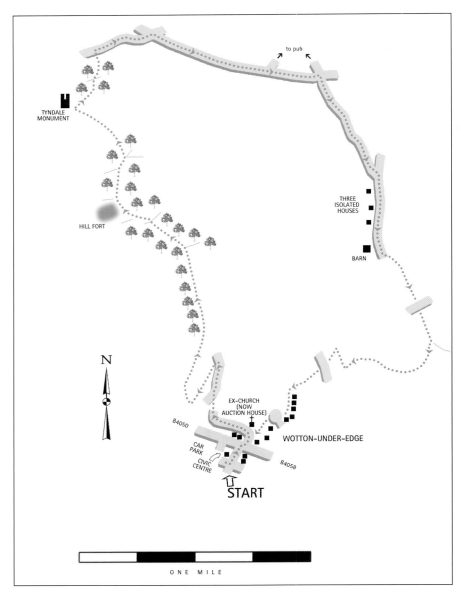

- In 300 yards, where a footpath crosses the road, turn left over a stile at a signpost to 'Wotton Hill'.

- Follow a track through the woods, initially swinging left (almost back upon yourself, with the road below to your left) before climbing to a stile.

- Cross the stile and follow a clear path ahead, leading through scrubland and then across open hillside to seats seen ahead beside a walled stand of trees.

Trees were originally planted here to commemorate the Battle of Waterloo in 1815. They were subsequently burnt to celebrate the end of the Crimean War in 1856, and replanted in 1887 for the Golden Jubilee of Queen Victoria.

- Walk around the enclosure and climb the path to a kissing gate, keeping the steep slope to your left.

- Go through the kissing gate and climb the slope for a yard or two, before turning left along a field edge, trees and a hedge on your left.

- At a cross-track at the far end of the field keep straight on, ignoring a turn into the woods at a National Trust sign.

- Continue along the path for half a mile, open fields through trees on your right and the edge on your left. When the field ends, at a T-junction, bear left and continue along the path, still with the edge on your left.

- Continue along a broad track, the edge on your left, ignoring side turns, for quarter of a mile, to a cross track with a broader track.

- Maintain your line of advance over the cross track (a broad blue and yellow arrow on a tree indicates the correct path; DO NOT turn left and descend the path marked with a single narrow yellow arrow).

- 120 yards later, fork right, still following the blue arrow.

In a few yards the ditch and ramparts of Blackenbury hill fort become visible, just to left of the path. This was one of the many hill forts that line the ridge of the Cotswolds. It covers four acres, and was constructed by digging a double ridge, with intervening ditch, across the neck of a spur of the Cotswolds ridge. This design, known as a 'promontory fort', is typical of the Cotswolds region, as is seen at its most spectacular at nearby Uley (see walk 2).

The entrance to the fort was not along the ridge, but up a hollow track climbing from the valley below, through the south-eastern side of the fort. The fort was not regularly occupied, but was constructed to provide an emergency shelter for the farmers who lived and worked in the Vale of Berkeley, who could move their families and animals up into the fort for protection if trouble loomed.

- Follow the track to a T-junction at the end of the ramparts.

If you wish to see the ramparts more closely, turn left and detour for 20 yards or so to see the double ditch and rampart.

- For the main walk, turn right at this T-junction and continue along the track, the edge again on your left.

- In a further 400 yards, turn right at a T-junction (the Tyndale monument can be glimpsed through the trees directly ahead) still following the blue arrows.

Tyndale monument.

- 100 yards further on, at a complex junction of paths, keep left (following blue arrows and yellow arrows) to a gate. Avoid losing height and keep the edge to your left.

- Go through the gate and follow the wide track through thinning trees to reach open grassland. Keep ahead, a fence on your left, to reach the Tyndale Monument.

This monument was erected in memory of William Tyndale in 1866. It stands 111 feet high on top of a 700 foot escarpment.

Tyndale was born in 1484, probably not in North Nibley as tradition has it, but more likely in the Welsh Marches. In 1524 Tyndale translated the New Testament into English, and also the Book of Jonah and the Pentateuch. His translation enabled his fellow countrymen to read the scriptures in their own language. It is upon this translation that the authorised bible, written by Miles Coverdale and published in 1539 under the name of Archbishop Cramner, was based.

Tyndale's relationship with Henry VIII was mixed. Tyndale came to the belief that the authority of Christianity rested with the scriptures and not the church, and that all men should be able to read the scriptures in their own language. When first expounded, this idea was far too radical for the king to accept. Gradually, as 'The King's Great Affair' (his divorce) dragged on and conflict with the Pope became more and more inevitable, Henry found intellectual arguments to convince himself that his course of action was correct, and gradually came around to Tyndale's position. Tyndale's publication of The Obedience of a Christian Man *in 1528 was taken by Henry as providing a moral justification for the king being the head of the Church in England. This was not precisely what Tyndale had said, and three years later Tyndale further opposed his king by demolishing Henry's theological arguments supporting his divorce. Tyndale was intellectually honest, and it was this honesty that led to his exile from England and his eventual execution.*

Tyndale's doctrines were to prove highly influential upon Henry's son Edward VI, far more of a protestant than his father ever was.

The monument can be climbed by obtaining the key from the house at the bottom of Wood Lane, at the end of the path that descends directly from the monument into

North Nibley. There are magnificent views from the top, across the Severn estuary and flood plain over to the Forest of Dean, although similar albeit lesser views can be seen standing at the tower's base.

- On leaving the monument, bear half-left, walking again with the edge on your left, soon dropping down a clear path into trees.

- Route finding for the next few hundred yards is complicated, and care in following the instructions precisely is urged.

- At a T-junction a few yards down the slope, bear right to maintain your line of advance.

- A few yards later descend into a sunken track. There is a waymarked gate to your right. DO NOT turn right through the gate, but bear to the left of it, ascending a clear, somewhat sunken path.

- At the top of the rise 75 yards later, bear half-left on to a narrow path leading into trees and apparently directly towards the edge (due north if you have a compass).

- Follow this path, soon with the edge on your left hand and shortly descending. Soon the path is enclosed between a fence and a hedge and descends steeply.

- Cross a fence and continue to descend the right-hand edge of a field to a stile.

- Cross the stile on to a lane and turn right.

- 600 yards along this lane, at a cross roads with a telephone box nearby, bear right (direction Waterley Bottom).

North Nibley is reputed, wrongly, to have been the birthplace of William Tyndale. It is also the site of last private battle fought in England. Ownership of the castle and estates of nearby Berkeley (see walk 11) was disputed after the death in 1417 of Thomas, Baron Berkeley, between his son-in-law and his nephew. The resulting feud continued for generations. In 1470, taking advantage of the breakdown in law and order caused by the Wars of the Roses, William Lord Berkeley (son of the nephew) and the Viscount de Lisle (grandson of the son-in-law) waged a private war with one another that culminated in the Battle of Nibley Green. The death of de Lisle at this battle, which cost 150 lives on both sides, effectively ended the dispute.

- Follow this quiet lane for 1,000 yards, to a side road on the left. If you wish to detour to the New Inn, turn left here for 500 yards, otherwise keep on along the main lane.

- In a further 500 yards, at a cross roads at the bottom of a hill, turn right, direction Wotton-under-Edge (the detour from the New Inn comes back in at this point).

- Continue along this attractive sunken lane, lined with wild garlic and overhanging shady trees, for half a mile. Ignore a footpath and bridle path joining from the left but continue up the lane for another half a mile, passing three isolated houses.

- Opposite a corrugated iron barn turn left into a waymarked bridleway. Soon bear right with the enclosed bridleway and climb steadily between fields.

- Climb through trees to a T-junction. Turn left and continue to climb to reach a lane.

- Cross the lane (the old London Road) and keep straight on along a track, a barn on your right.

- Follow the track as it narrows to a footpath. Just after it starts to descend, cross a waymarked stile on the right.

- Curve right with the path, keeping a wall close on your right hand and with the valley far below to your left.

- Follow the path as it curves around a spur and then curves back right, across the head of a valley.

As you turn the corner, ridges can clearly be seen running around the slope opposite. These are strip lynchets, the remains of earthen mounds dug in the Middle Ages. These were often used to demark the boundaries of individuals holdings within a larger communal field within which strip farming was practiced. The lynchets you see here were used by Kingswood Abbey, which stood nearby until the Dissolution of the Monastries 1536-9, as a vineyard.

- Continue to follow the top of the slope. At telegraph wires, where the slope levels out, turn right and follow a fence uphill to cross a stile beside a gate.

- Continue ahead, a fence and hedge on your right. Follow the path into woods and 100 yards later turn sharp left downhill, turning back upon your left.

- Descend the path, initially keeping a fence on your left hand, but fork right downhill before reaching a gate and a stile across the path.

- Descend the steep narrow path through trees to reach a stile above a house. Follow stepped, enclosed path down to a lane.

- Turn left down the lane for 50 yards and then turn right through a kissing gate.

- Pass between seats and follow a clear path downhill to pass to the right of houses below.

- Turn left and follow an enclosed path behind the houses.

- Pass concrete posts and keep ahead along a fenced alley to emerge at the head of a cul-de-sac.

- Keep ahead up an alley towards the church seen ahead.

- Pass along the side of the church and keep straight on down the road back to the main road and your start.

Walk 16

Sudeley Castle and Queen Catherine Parr

Distance: 4 miles

Map: OS 163

Start and parking: The walk starts at the free car park in Back Lane, Winchcombe (grid ref: 024284). Winchcombe is on the B4632, six miles north of Cheltenham on the road to Stratford-upon-Avon. The car park, behind the Library, is signposted from the town centre.

Refreshments: Public houses, shops and tea rooms in Winchcombe.

Historical Background

Sudeley Castle was the last home and final resting place of Catherine Parr, Henry VIII's sixth wife. Catherine was one of the most influential women of the Tudor era, a time when the role of upper-class women was altering dramatically. They were expected to be able managers of their husband's estates, leading to a demand for better education and greater political skills. The Tudor Court, initially under Henry VII's mother Margaret Beaufort, and later under Henry VIII's first wife Catherine of Aragon, became the centre for a group of intellectual and articulate women who were at the centre of promoting the 'New Learning', the Humanist ideals of Eramus that formed the basis of the Reformation (see walk 15).

The Parr family were rich and influential northern landlords and courtiers. Catherine was born in 1512, and educated as a child in Henry VIII's court. At nine she was married to the elderly Lord Borough. On his early death six years later she returned to court a rich widow, to become maid-of-honour to Queen Catherine. The next few years confirmed Catherine as a staunch humanist, with a zeal for reforming religion. In 1531 she married again, this time to the powerful northern baron Lord Latimer. Much of the next decade was spent on the Latimer estates, and Catherine was able to observe but avoid the political turmoil in court. Lord Latimer's reluctant involvement in the northern revolt known as the Pilgrimage of Grace earned him the enmity of Thomas Cromwell, and Catherine used her influence with the king (who had been her friend and patron since she was a child) to help bring about Cromwell's downfall.

By 1543, when Henry was seeking a sixth wife, Catherine had become an obvious choice. She was the wealthiest woman in England, strongly connected with powerful families who were politically unaligned, a woman moreover whom the king knew well and liked and whose judgement he respected. As queen, Catherine was a great support to Henry in his last years, reconciling him to his estranged daughter Mary, and diverting him from his illnesses. Catherine was also an able politician, acting as Henry's regent during his absence in the French wars, and promoting Humanism and a moderate middle way in the Reformation. She had observed and learnt from the errors of Anne Boleyn and Catherine Howard, and used this knowledge to great affect in avoiding a dangerous plot by the Catholic faction in Court to unseat her.

Catherine's power ended in 1547 with the death of Henry and the accession of the young Edward VI. Inexplicably, she allowed herself to be rapidly wooed and married to Thomas Seymour, younger brother of the Lord Protector, and retired to his estate at Sudeley. Here she was joined by Princess Elizabeth. During the next 17 months the future queen learnt much of the art of politics from one of the Tudor Era's great political survivors. In 1548 Catherine died, at the age of 36, of puerperal fever after giving birth to her only child.

The Walk

This walk starts in the historic market town of Winchcombe and climbs gently on to rolling hills before descending to Sudeley Castle and Park. Directions need to be followed carefully in the middle section of the walk.

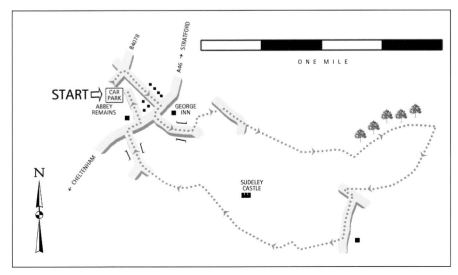

- Leave the car park and turn right along Back Lane, back towards the town centre.

- At the cross roads, turn right into North Street.

- Go along North Street to a T-junction. Cross the road to the inn sign (St George) and peep down the alleyway to see the former George Inn opposite.

The George Inn was once a coaching inn, but before that it had been built as a hostel for pilgrims travelling to Winchcombe Abbey, which was second only to Canterbury as a destination for pilgrimage in the Middle Ages. Above the door of the inn are the initials 'R K', standing for Richard Kydderminster, the last Abbot of Winchcombe, who died before he could witness the dissolution of the Abbey.

- Facing the George, turn right along the High Street, passing the Tourist Information Centre on the corner opposite.

- Take the first turn on the left, down Castle Street.

- Follow the road over a bridge and 30 yards later, turn left into a footpath between houses.

- Go through a kissing gate into a field. IGNORE an obvious footpath going straight on but instead go half-right, to a wooden kissing gate beside a field gate on the far side of the field.

- Go through the gate into a lane and turn right. Where the lane bends right, at the end of a high wall, go left through a field gate at a footpath sign.

- Go half-right across the field, aiming just to the side of a telegraph pole in mid-field, to reach a gap in the hedge, 50 yards to the left of a gateway.

- Cross a plank bridge and turn left, to follow the field edge to a waymarked gate.

- Maintain your line of advance across the next, third, field to a gap in the hedge, halfway along the opposite field edge.

- Maintain your line of advance across the fourth field, to reach the corner of a fence ahead. Pass around the corner and continue along the fence, keeping the fence close on your left hand, to a stile in the top left-hand corner of the field. (The stile can be obscured by undergrowth in summer.)

- Cross the stile and head up the slope, keeping the fence on your left, to reach a stile beside a gate at the top of the field.

There is a good view of Sudeley Castle below you.

- Cross the stile and go up the field, a fence and wood on your left, to a gate at the top of the field.

- Go through the gate and curve right, keeping the woods immediately on your left hand.

- Cross a stile in the top corner of the field and keep ahead, the woods still on your left hand, to cross a second stile 20 yards later.

- Keep ahead, the woods still immediately on your left, to a stile beside a metal field gate.

- DO NOT cross the stile but turn sharp right back on yourself. Go steeply downhill, gradually converging with the hedge on your left. Eventually a metal field gate, hidden in a dip, comes into sight on your left. (DO NOT aim for a gate constantly visible in the bottom of the field: your target is hidden in the dip to its left.)

- Go through the gate and along a clear track, to reach a stile beside a second gate.

- Cross the stile and keep ahead along a grassy track for 15 yards. Where the track bends left to go up in front of a house, go QUARTER-RIGHT down the field, aiming to the left of farm buildings below. There is no path across this field, but soon a waymarked stile comes into sight ahead.

- Cross the stile and keep ahead, aiming to the right of an oak tree ahead.

- Past the tree veer left to a stile beside a gate in the field corner.

- Cross the stile and turn left and left again, to go up a road. In 50 yards turn right along a No Through Road, signed 'Sudeley Lodge Parks Farm'.

- Follow the lane for 300 yards. Opposite a house on the left, and at a sign saying 'Private Drive Public Footpath', turn right through a gate.

- Go down the field, a hedge on your right hand, to a stile in the bottom corner.

- Cross the stile and turn right. Follow the field boundary, a fence on your right, to a metal field gate.

- DO NOT go through the gate but turn left along the edge of the field to a stile in the corner.

- Cross the stile and keep ahead for 10 yards to cross a second stile on your right.

You are now entering the park of Sudeley Castle. From the time of the Saxon King Ethelred (the Unready) Sudeley was a royal estate, and included a well-stocked deer park, running from where you are now standing, for several miles up the valley to the south. There was a small hunting lodge where the castle now stands.

- Go half-left across the park, aiming for a marker post.

Ahead can be seen the free-standing chapel of Sudeley Castle, St Mary's Chapel, built originally in 1450 but faithfully restored in the last century. Catherine Parr was buried there and her stone coffin is still in the chapel.

- Continue your line of advance to the next marker post and then continue ahead towards the corner of the fence ahead, the castle in front and to your right.

The first small castle was built, illegally, by Lord de Sudeley around 1140, to provide protection for his estates during the turbulent reign of King Stephen. The initial castle was small, little more than a fortified manor, and it remained such for the next three centuries.

Sudeley castle.

In 1367 William, Lord Boteler, married Joan de Sudeley, and upon her father's death, inherited the castle and estates. William's son Ralph, became Lord Chamberlain to Henry IV was created Baron Sudeley, and his son Thomas was Admiral of the Fleet under Henry VI and amassed a fortune fighting the French. Thomas used his money to rebuild Sudeley Castle on a far grander scale between 1440-50, with an inner and an outer courtyard, an impressively substantial keep, and a fine chapel and tithe barn.

The next Boteler, Ralph, was an ardent Lancastrian during the Wars of the Roses, and his estates were confiscated and given to Richard of Gloucester (later Richard III), who rebuilt the eastern side of the inner courtyard as a splendid state apartment. Sudeley remained a royal castle throughout the reigns of Henry VII and Henry VIII, but Edward VI gave the castle to his Lord High Admiral, Thomas Seymour, who lived here with his wife, Catherine Parr, and with Princess Elizabeth, the future queen.

Seymour was jealous of his brother the Royal Protector, and attempted to kidnap the young king in order to enhance his position. He was executed for treason and the castle passed to Catherine's brother William, who in turn was executed in 1554 for his part in Wyatt's rebellion against Queen Mary. Mary gave the castle to a loyal supporter, Sir John Brydges, the first Lord Chandos, who rebuilt the outer courtyard as a residence rather than a stronghold, with the wide mullioned windows seen today. It was Sir John's son who, as constable of the Tower of London, deliberately delayed the execution of Mary's death warrant on her sister Elizabeth, thereby saving the future queen's life and earning her gratitude.

The sixth Lord Chandos held the castle for Charles I during the Civil War, and raised his own regiment to fight for the king. In 1642 parliamentary forces from Gloucester captured the castle, and garrisoned it for 18 months until Lord Chandos eventually recaptured it. The castle was 'slighted', that is, its defences destroyed, at the end of the Civil war.

Sudeley was left as a ruin for 200 years, before being bought in 1863 by John and William Dent, brothers and local glove makers, who restored part of the house and the chapel. The formal gardens were laid out by their niece, Emma Dent, who was enthusiastically involved in both restoring the castle and forging close links with the town of Winchcombe. Almshouses renovated by Emma will be seen later in the walk.

Sudeley Castle is open beginning of April–end of October, 11am–5.30pm. There is an admission charge.

- At the corner of the fence keep ahead, the fence close on your right, to a kissing gate.

- Pass the kissing gate and keep ahead to go through a second kissing gate.

- Keep ahead along a broad fenced path, an adventure playground on your left and the castle on your right.

- At the end of the path, go through a gate and over a drive, passing through a second gate and back into the park.

- Keep straight on to a wooden kissing gate beside a large oak.

- Maintain your line of advance across the end of the park to go through a metal kissing gate beside trees.

- Follow the fence down to a drive and turn right across an ornamental bridge.

- Continue along the chestnut-lined drive to pass the gatehouse and join a lane.

- Continue ahead along the lane, over a bridge.

This lane was formerly known as Duck Street, since there was a ducking stool at the river in the Middle Ages. This was a common instrument of punishment, whereby a 'scold', or an offensively sharp-tongued woman of the community, was tied to a stool and ducked in the river, to force her to adopt behaviour more acceptable to her neighbours.

- Follow the lane to a T-junction.

- Turn right into the market square.

On the left is Dent Terrace, a row of almshouses. The first almshouses here were founded in 1573 by Lady Chandos, wife to the third Lord, to house the 'poor and needy' of their parish of Sudeley. The terrace was renovated in 1887, and at the same time the town's first regular water supply was laid on. Both deeds were the work of Emma Dent, by then the owner of Sudeley Castle after the death of her husband.

- At the end of the square, cross the road and turn left into Cowl Lane.

Winchcombe Abbey once stood behind the high wall on the left. Winchcombe was the capital of King Kenulf, who founded the Abbey in 811 AD, in memory of his son Kenelm. Kenelm, a seven-year-old boy designated by Kenulf as his heir, was murdered by his own sister Quendrida, who herself had aspirations on the crown. In reparation an existing nunnery, founded 25 years earlier by Kenulf's predecessor Offa, was redeveloped as an elaborate Abbey, and given to the Benedictines to tend. The Abbey grew to great wealth, partly by shrewd investment in land and sheep rearing, and partly due to Kenelm's elevation to sainthood, which made Winchcombe into a place of pilgrimage second only to Canterbury. In 1539 the Abbey was confiscated under the Dissolution, and its land put into the hands of local commissioners who were responsible for its sale. The leading commissioner was Lord Seymour of Sudeley, who bought the best of the Abbey's land himself. Within a few years nothing remained of the Abbey, even its stones being removed to build local houses. The stone coffins of Kenulf and Kenelm did survive however, and are today in St Peter's Church.

- A short detour to the left will take you to St Peters, the building of which was in part funded by Sir Ralph Botoler of Sudeley. The tower still bears the marks of Civil War cannon-balls, fired in 1642 when Parliament was attacking Sudeley Castle.

- To continue the walk, go along Cowl Lane for 150 yards and then turn left back into the car park.

Walk 17

Danby Lodge and the management of the Forest of Dean

Distance: 5 miles

Map: OS 162

Start and parking: This walk starts from the Wench Ford picnic area in Blakeneyhill Woods (grid ref: 653082). The picnic area is clearly marked from the junction of two minor roads in the middle of the Forest of Dean, one which runs one mile southwards from Upper Soudley joining another which winds from Parkend to Nibley (near Blakeney). Car parking is free.

Refreshments: None on route.

Historical Background

As the climate improved after the end of the last Ice Age, trees started to return to the British Isles – 53 species established themselves as native to Britain, in huge forests covering much of the country. The Forest of Dean grew to cover 120,000 acres, with oak as the predominant species.

Around 4000 BC farmers moved in and started to clear the forest, for arable land, building material, and to aid hunting. By the Iron Age (around 700 BC) man had discovered how to work with metals, and the iron ore resources of the forest, located in an arc from Staunton to Lydney, started to be exploited, a process accelerated during Roman times. Large areas of the forest were cleared for mining. Charcoal was an essential component of the iron smelting process, and demand for charcoal led to further deforestation.

Although the demand for wood and iron led to a steady contraction of the Forest of Dean, the strict control of the forests natural resources imposed by the Norman monarchs resulted in the forest remaining largely intact (see walk 7). This altered in the early 17th century, when James I allowed private entrepreneurs to remove minerals on a grand scale in return for payment to the crown, or 'royalty'. From 1620 onwards there was massive deforestation, exacerbated during the Civil War, when the royalist Sir John Wyntour (or Winter), the major land rentier in the area, destroyed his mines and plantations rather than risk their falling into Parliamentary hands. By 1667 there were only 200 oaks left in the whole forest.

To halt this wholesale destruction of natural resources of the royal forest, Charles II passed the Dean Forest (Reforestation) Act in 1668. This resulted in the extensive replanting of over 11,000 acres of trees, mainly oak, in six huge plantations. Lodges such as Danby Lodge were built to house officials responsible for managing the Forest. At the same time the Court of Verderers, an ancient council established by the Normans to manage the 'vert (wood and vegetation) and venison' in the Forest, was revitalised, and a new meeting house for the council built at Speech House. This was soon extended to manage the mineral resources of the Forest as well.

The Walk

This walk is entirely within the Forest of Dean on footpaths and tracks, and passes many features illustrating the Forest's rich past. The route undulates, with occasional short, steep climbs, but is generally not strenuous.

The approach road to the picnic site is part of the trackway of the Forest of Dean Central Railway. It initially carried no passengers, only freight, and was built in 1809 to serve the coal industry of the Forest, hauling coal and iron ore to the docks on the Severn at Lydney. It originally operated as a horse-drawn tramway until 1868 when it was upgraded as a broad gauge steam railway. The railway was not a commercial success, only generating enough traffic to justify one train every second day. It was used as a passenger service until 1929, then reverted to freight only, and was finally closed in 1976.

● From the toilet block, cross the trackway and descend the ramp to the picnic area, signed 'Start of forest walk'.

● Go forward to the river bank and turn left. Ignore a footbridge in a few yards but continue along the bank, river on your right.

The trees here are mainly oak, planted during the reign of Charles II to replenish the Forest. The demand for wood continued to grow however, as the expansion of the British Navy from the Commonwealth era onwards led to an insatiable demand of oak. Demand for the forests resources was accelerated dramatically by the Napoleonic Wars, and in 1808 Lord Glenbervie, Surveyor General at the Office of Woods, responded to worries in the Admiralty by passing another Enclosure Act, designed specifically to produce Oak for the navy. Between 1810 and 1819 30 million acorns were planted in the Forest, and by 1840 another 20,000 acres had been replanted, mainly with oak.

Unfortunately, oak production is a long term investment, with trees ideally not being

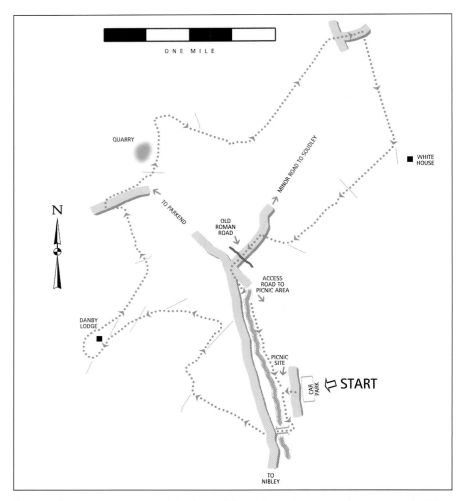

ONE MILE

QUARRY

TO PARKEND

MINOR ROAD TO SOUDLEY

WHITE HOUSE

N

OLD ROMAN ROAD

ACCESS ROAD TO PICNIC AREA

DANBY LODGE

PICNIC SITE

CAR PARK

⇩ START

TO NIBLEY

harvested for 120-50 years, and by the middle of the 19th century the navy was building its ships of iron. Interest in preserving the Forest declined, and the woods were allowed to deteriorate. With World War One demand for wood increased again, this time for charcoal to produce cordite (an essential component in explosive shells), and acetone (used in camouflage paint). Again the resources of the forest were severely attacked, and this deterioration continued until after World War II, when the newly established Forestry Commission was charged with preserving the Forest of Dean. Extensive replanting resulted, until today the forest covers 27,000 acres, 27 percent of the trees are oak, with beech, ash and sweet chestnut also plentiful.

● In 250 yards, turn right over a stone bridge.

- Go half-right across the road and then turn left on to a footpath leading into the woods (a post marks the entrance spot).

- In a few yards fork right and gently climb with a broad path into the trees.

Around the picnic site the trees were predominantly oaks, the traditional tree of the Forest of Dean. Here they are conifers, larch, spruce and fir, late arrivals planted as a cash crop.

Although oak was the most sought-after tree in the forest, the steady growth in demand for iron led to softer woods being grown for conversion into charcoal. Iron ore was heated in charcoal ovens at 300-50 degrees centigrade for 24 hours in order to produce molten metal suitable for working, and the insatiable demand for iron led to the forest being denuded of softwood trees as well as hardwoods. Fast growing softwoods were reintroduced into the Forest during the reign of Charles II to cope with this demand.

- On reaching a broad track, turn right.

- Follow the track downhill for a quarter of a mile, around a left-hand bend and then around a sharp right-hand bend.

- After climbing the next rise, at a red waymark post, turn left on to a footpath that initially runs parallel to the track, but after 100 yards or so turns left up into the woods.

- At the top of the slope, where a path joins from the right, bear left and continue, the path initially flatter but soon climbing briefly again to a cross track.

- Go over the cross track and continue up the footpath, climbing steeply to reach another cross track.

- Turn left along the cross track, the wall around Danby Lodge visible on the right.

- In 100 yards ignore a fork to the left but continue to follow the right-hand path, keeping the wall on your right.

- On reaching a wide track turn right, still with the boundary fence of Danby Lodge on your right.

The mounds to the left are the remains of a 'free mine'. Miners born in the Hundred of St Briavels, a Norman administrative area roughly equivalent to today's Forest of Dean, who were sons of miners and had worked in a mine for one year and a day, were granted the right to mine coal completely independently by the Norman crown (see walk 7). Until the 18th century these 'free miners' had the sole right to extract iron ore, and later coal, within the Royal Forest, although the minerals extracted were still the property of the Crown. The free miners owned small mines throughout the forest, and were free to sell any of the iron or coal they extracted on the open market, in return for paying the royal owners of those minerals a fee, or 'royalty'.

Coal became very important in Victorian times, with up to 1 million tons a year ripped out, mainly by open cast mining. Demand for Dean coal had largely ended by the 1930s, when deep shaft mining in South Wales and Northern England was generating greater output more economically. Some free mining continued, often on a cottage industry basis. Today there are three full-time free miners still working the forest, and seven part-time miners. Hopewell Colliery near Speech House is a free mine, open to the public Easter-October, where the free miner who owns and works the mine gives personal and fascinating tours.

- Pass the gates of Danby Lodge and continue ahead past a horse barrier.
- 20 yards past the barrier, turn right again, still with the wall on your right.

On your right are more spoil heaps and 'scowles', abandoned surface workings of free mines that have gradually been reclaimed by the forest. Up to a dozen mines currently operate in the forest at any one time, producing 'small coal' used for fuelling power stations. This is generally sold at the pithead to local purchasers.

- Soon pass Danby Lodge.

In 1667 Charles II reimposed strict control over the resources of the Royal Forest of Dean, halting the neglect and exploitation allowed by his father and grandfather. A number of full-time foresters were employed, who lived in the forest and were responsible for overseeing the replanting of trees and managing both forestry and hunting. Six lodges were built within the forest itself to accommodate these royal foresters, one to administer each of the six 'walks' or plantations into which the forest was divided. Danby Lodge is one such lodge, named after Charles Danby, Viscount Latimer, an important local landowner.

At the same time a new meeting house, Speech House, was built for the revitalised Court of Verderers, the ancient council established by King Cnut to manage the 'vert (wood and vegetation) and venison' in the forest. It was soon recognised that mineral resources were also important and required management, and free miners were allowed to sit in the council and participate in the management of the forest.

The re-organisation of the forest by Charles II was deeply resented by the local population, who rightly foresaw that the reforestation programme and the restrictions upon tree-felling for charcoal would adversely affect the local iron industry (see walk 18). There were riots in 1688, and two lodges, Worcester and York Lodges, were severely damaged.

- Continue ahead from the Lodge down a grassy track, to reach a cross track.
- Turn left and follow the cross track, drops to your right and wide views opening up over the forest.

You soon pass a prominent outcrop of quartz, known locally as the 'Jesus rock', from which there are fine views over the forest to the east.

- After half a mile, the track curves away from the edge and descends to a broad sandy cross track.
- Go over the cross track and go half-left down a footpath (marked with a red waymark) through trees. Ignore side turns and continue downhill.

- At a cross track, with the road visible below through the trees, turn left and follow the path before turning right at a waymark sign and descending to the road (continuing a little, and then zigzagging left and then right will avoid a very steep final descent).

- On reaching the road, turn right for 30 yards and then cross the road and go over a stile and footbridge, at a red waymarker. (If you did not zigzag but descended directly down the slope, cross directly over the road to reach this stile.)

- Turn right along the banks of the stream.

- In 100 yards, at a bridge on the right, turn left over a stile and then immediately turn right to resume your line of advance, parallel to the stream and road on your right.

- The broad path soon starts to climb gently and swings left to join a cross track.

- Turn right along the track for 10 yards, and then turn left over a stile. Keep ahead up a grassy path, soon passing an old quarry on the left.

Note the old coppicing of trees on your left. The process of coppicing was developed by Stone Age farmers, who moved into the forest from around 4000 BC, cutting trees with flint implements for fuel and building material. Coppicing was developed as a timber-management technique, with trees being felled and new shoots allowed to grow from the bases. These new shoots were cultivated to produce all manner of tools.

- At a fork in the path bear right (still waymarked in red), climbing steadily to reach a broad sandy track.

- Turn right along the track, ignoring side turns to the left and soon with views over the forest on your right.

This track is called the Blakeney Straits, part of an extensive tramway system built in the forest between 1800 and 1812, to link industrial and mining sites with the waterways of the Severn and Wye, and hence with the rest of the country. Tramways were quickly and cheaply constructed, following natural contours around slopes and avoiding tunnels and bridges. They consisted of cast iron rails resting on stone blocks, along which wagons were pulled by horses. After 1850 many of the tramways were upgraded into railways, along which steam locomotives were able to draw far greater loads. Often however (as was the case with the Central Railway seen at the start of this walk), the technology was introduced because it was available rather than because it was needed, since mine and foundry output often did not justify the increased freight capacity provided.

- Descend with the track. In half a mile ignore a waymarked footpath to the right and continue along the track.

- Soon ignore two stiles on the right in quick succession. Follow the track to a metal gate.

- By-pass the gate using a stile on the right and follow the track out to a road.

Roman road in Forest of Dean.

- Cross the road and keep straight on along the side road opposite, signed 'Bradley Hill'.

- In 75 yards, turn right on to a Forestry Commission road, signed 'No unauthorised vehicles'.

- Follow the track, descending and then climbing again.

- After nearly half a mile, at the top of a rise and just as a white house comes into view ahead, turn right down a broad grassy track.

Sheep can often be seen grazing the forest here. The free miners not only worked in the forest but lived in it, some in disused mines and caves, most in substantial stone cottages surrounded by a small garden for the production of vegetables, and a hen-coop or pig-sty. Under their ancient rights, the free miners were entitled to some of the natural product of the Royal Forest in which they lived – timber and firewood, berries and roots for their own consumption, acorns for their pigs. To the free miner, these rights extended also to the grazing of their sheep in the forest. This extension was opposed by the Crown, and was subject to bitter disputes in the Court of Verderers. Finally the Crown had to concede and the right of grazing is now defined. The sheep seen grazing the forest today are the product of that far-off dispute.

- Go over a sandy cross track and continue along the grassy track, which curves gradually right and then descends to a surfaced track.

- Turn right through a horse barrier and descend to the road.

- Turn left along the road and cross a bridge over a brook.

- Follow the road towards an ex-railway arch.

On the right of the road, between the river and the railway arch, you can see a section of old Roman road. The Romans advanced across the Severn into the Forest of Dean in 70 AD, and iron production was rapidly put under military control. Iron foundries were built at Lydney and Cinderford, with military garrisons to protect them, and a series of roads built into the forest, to enable both iron ore and if necessary troops to be moved rapidly. By the third century, the Roman frontier was secure along the Wye, and iron production expanded dramatically, and with it the network of roads through the forest.

- Pass under the railway arch and turn left into the access road to the picnic site.

- Do not go along the road but just before the gate into the site, by a sign displaying closing times, descend a path to the right, leading to the brook.

- At the brook bank turn left and follow a path, the brook on your right, back to the picnic site.

Walk 18

Coleford: industry in the Forest of Dean

Distance: 5 miles

Map: OS 162

Start and parking: This walk starts from the clock tower in the centre of Coleford (grid ref: 575107). Coleford is on the B4228, four miles east of Monmouth along the A4136. There is plentiful free parking in Coleford, particularly in a large car park close to the Tourist Information Office.

Refreshments: Shops and public houses in Coleford and in Clearwell, tea rooms at Clearwell Caves.

Historical Background

Iron has been extracted from the Forest of Dean since the Iron Age, when the Siluries tribe mined the ore and exported it, not only throughout England but to Europe as well. The rich iron ore deposits of the forest were a major factor in the decision of the Romans to move on from their original frontier along the Cotswold ridge and advance into Wales. The Romans made the Wye their frontier, and criss-crossed the forest with roads (see walk 17), connecting mines and forges deep in the woods with their main port of Lydney on the Bristol Channel.

The forest remained an active iron working area throughout the Saxon era, but it was under the Normans that the industry expanded massively, until by the late 13th century there were some 70 forges producing 150 tons of iron a year, one sixth of England's total production. The Normans administered the forest from St Briavels (see walk 7), but mining was done by the free miners, inhabitants of the forest with jealously guarded traditional rights (see walk 17). Ancient methods of smelting and forging were gradually replaced with blast furnaces, and by the Civil War the forest had the greatest concentration of iron foundries in the country. By 1717, 5,000 tons of pig iron a year was being produced in the region.

Traditionally, the abundant woodlands of the forest meant that furnaces had burnt charcoal, but wholesale deforestation led Charles II to impose strict controls over the amount of trees felled (see walk 17). This led the industry to alternative fuel, namely coal, also plentiful in the forest. When the iron industry declined in the 19th century, the traditional mining skills were redeployed into coal mining. By 1856, 220 mines were producing 600,000 tons of coal a year, and at its peak, just before World War Two, the forest was producing 1,300,000 tons annually.

After the war the mining industry in the forest went into terminal decline, and today it is hard to believe that once this was one of the leading mining areas in Britain. The names of many of the towns, such as Cinderford and Coleford, still give echoes of that industrial past, and many examples of the regions industrial history are still to be found around the town of Coleford.

The Walk

This walk is predominantly across fields, offering extensive views over the Wye Valley and the Forest of Dean whilst visiting several relics of the town's history as a centre of the iron industry. While the walk is not over strenuous it does undulate for much of its route.

- Facing the clock tower, with your back to the zebra crossing, turn left down the road signed 'Newland 2'.

The traffic island now providing the base for the clock tower was originally called the Tump and was the market place of old Coleford. A chapel stood on the site of the clock tower since at least 1489, and regular markets were held around it, to which local farmers brought their produce, to trade and to sell to the inhabitants of the growing town. By then Coleford was already the centre of the iron processing industry, which had reached its peak in the 13th century. It was also the centre for the mining of coal, a mineral whose uses were increasingly recognised, and in 1282 was named 'Coleford'. Charles II gave the town its charter, in recognition of its continued importance as an iron and coal producer.

The original medieval chapel was replaced by a larger one in 1821. This later chapel was demolished in 1882 and today only the tower remains.

- Soon pass toilets on the left and 20 yards later turn right up Bowen Hill.

- Follow the road as it winds uphill. Pass Angel Field on the left and 30 yards later, opposite Boxbush Road, turn left through a kissing gate into an enclosed footpath.

- Follow the footpath gently uphill to emerge on to a road.

- Turn left through the gates of a recreation ground. Follow the drive past a childrens' play area.

- After 50 yards, at a junction of footpaths, bear left with the drive, with the play area and bowling green to the left and football pitch to the right.

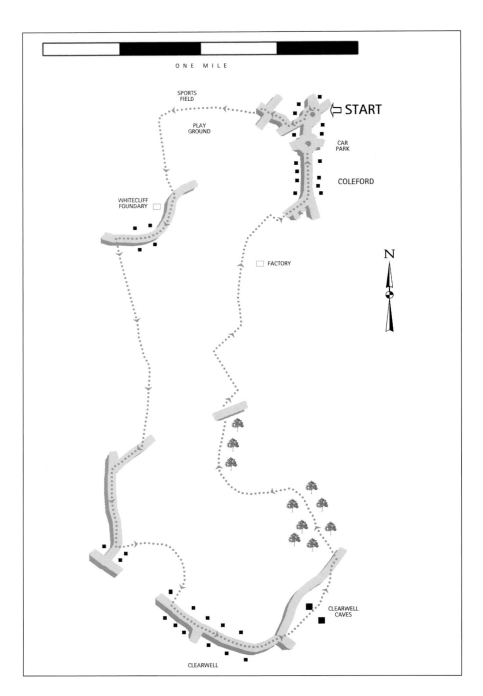

ONE MILE

SPORTS FIELD

PLAY GROUND

⇦ START

CAR PARK

COLEFORD

WHITECLIFF FOUNDARY

FACTORY

N

CLEARWELL CAVES

CLEARWELL

- Where the drive forks, just past a house on the left, keep straight on. A few yards later, just before metal posts, turn left and walk along a track to a gate, leading into a field.

- Go half-right across the field to a stile beside a telegraph pole on the opposite side of the field.

- Cross the stile and keep straight on, a hedge close on your right hand, to a ruined gate in the bottom right corner.

- Go down an enclosed path on to a track.

- Go half-right across the track, through a gate opposite into a field.

- Turn immediately left and descend the field to an opening at the bottom boundary.

Note the old kiln passed on the left, part of the nearby Whitcliff Foundry.

- Go through the opening and turn right down the field to cross a stile leading on to a road.

- Turn right along the road, passing the ruins of Whitcliff Foundry on your right in 100 yards.

The Whitcliff Furnace was built around 1800, and is an example of an early coke-fired

Blast furnace, Whitcliff Foundry.

blast furnace, used for making iron. Work on the original furnace, a venture of local businessmen, started around 1797, but before it was completed it was swept away in a flash flood following heavy snows and the subsequent thaw. The project was taken over by James Teague and commenced operation three years later.

In 1810 David Mushet, a Scot and a pioneer in the developing iron industry, came to Coleford to take over the running of the Whitcliff Furnace. His son, Robert Forester Mushet, followed his father into the iron trade, and discovered the process of alloying iron, manganese, silicon and carbon, thereby turning molten pig iron into steel. This revolutionary process, the basis of modern steel-making, was first used here at the Whitcliff Foundry. Mushet started to patent his process, but failed to maintain stamp duties on his patents, which lapsed. Subsequently the same process was discovered by Henry Bessemer, who did patent the work, and whose name is now forever associated with the process previously used here at Whitcliff.

- Continue along this quiet road, passing the entrance to Whitcliff quarry. Continue, passing houses, for 600 yards, to a bridleway sign by a gate on the left.

- Go through the gate and climb to a stile 20 yards later. Cross the stile and keep straight on, up the left-hand side of a long field.

- Cross a stile in the top left-hand corner of the field and continue ahead along a shady footpath, a fence on your right.

- Cross a stile and maintain your line of advance up the next field. DO NOT go through an open gateway in the middle of the top field boundary, but instead go through a metal gate just to its left and behind. (You are thus entering the left-hand most of two adjoining fields.)

- Keep ahead down the right-hand field boundary.

- Pass into the next field and immediately turn left. Walk along the field with a line of trees on your left hand. Turn right with the field boundary, to an opening on the left, halfway down the field.

- Go through the opening and keep ahead to a gate in the opposite side of the field, leading into a lane.

- Turn right down the quiet lane to reach the outskirts of Clearwell in 800 yards.

- Just before reaching a farm on the left, turn left over a stile and go half-left up the field to a stile opposite.

- Go over the stile and maintain your line of advance to a stile at the top of the field.

- Go half-right up this third field, to a gap in the hedge on the right-hand side, 60 yards up from the bottom corner of the field.

- Go through the gap and cross the next field to a stile into a track.

- Cross the track and go half-right up the field opposite.

- Follow the right-hand boundary fence through a line of trees and up to a gate in the top right-hand corner. AVOID an obvious waymarked stile five yards to the left of the gate.

- Cross a stile beside the gate and keep forward, the fence on your right side. Follow the fence around to a right-hand corner and downhill to a stile beside a gate.

- Cross the stile and continue downhill on an enclosed path, to a stile on to a road.

- Turn left on the road (the shop is just to your right), passing the Wyndham Arms on your right (one of Clearwell's two public houses).

- Bear left at the war memorial, signed 'Clearwell Caves', passing the Butchers Arms.

- Follow the road for 400 yards. After the last house on the right, where the pavement ends, continue ahead along a clear footpath along the top of a grassy bank to the right of the road, to reach Clearwell Caves, the tea rooms on your left, and the entrance to your right.

Iron ore has been extracted from Clearwell Caves since 500 BC. Iron from these caves was one of the basic items of trade upon which the economy of the Siluries, the original Iron Age tribe who inhabited this area, was based. The caverns are a natural cave system that became filled with iron ore deposits, the removal of which over the centuries resulted in labyrinth of tunnels and chambers.

Mining was originally done by hand, but as the miners went deeper in pursuit of iron ore seams fire-setting was used. This involved lighting fires and dousing them with water in order to crack the rock. Once extracted, iron ore was smelted in furnaces up to 24 hours at temperatures of 300-350 degrees to product molten metal. Their furnaces were fuelled by charcoal, itself produced by burning the wood found in abundance in the local forest. The resulting iron was molded into blocks or 'pigs', and then traded.

The iron ore deposits of the Forest of Dean attracted the Romans into the area after the invasion, and were systematically mined in one of the most active periods of the caves history iron ore. The resulting pig iron was exported across the Empire.

By the 13th century there were up to 72 active furnaces in the forests surrounding Coleford, needing ever increasing amounts of wood: 5,000 cubic feet of timber were needed for each iron bar produced. Deforestation upon a massive scale resulted. The mines went ever deeper in pursuit of the ore, the deepest levels being 500 feet. The ore was mined by free miners and carried to the surface by boys of 12 years old, half a hundredweight at a time.

By the 17th century the navy was becoming deeply concerned about the loss of hardwoods, especially oak, needed for ship building. Under pressure from the Admiralty, severe restrictions were placed upon the removal of wood (see walk 17). This crippled the local iron industry, which declined severely until the 19th century, when coke was discovered as an alternative source of fuel. By then however, there was competition from other iron producing areas, and although it went on producing iron until 1945, the local industry never really recovered.

Today eight main caverns or 'churns' are open to public, and also house a museum of working life.

Clearwell Caves are open 1 March–31 October, daily, 10am–5pm. Admission charge.

- From the tea rooms continue uphill to reach the car park.
- Turn left down the access road to reach the main road.
- Turn right along the road for 100 yards and then turn left across a stile.
- Go along a wide footpath to another stile.

Just before this stile, look left: there is the entrance to an ochre mine, partially hidden in the roots of a large tree. This ochre mine was small scale mining venture of an individual free miner.

Mining within the Forest of Dean was historically the prerogative of the free miners. To be a free miner, a man needs to have been born within the Hundred of St Briavels (the Norman administrative area roughly covering the modern Forest of Dean), the son of a miner, and to have worked in the mines for a year and a day. The free miners were a self-governing body, with rights and privileges granted by the Crown, including the exclusive right to mine all the iron and later coal extracted from the royal forest. The ore extracted remained the property of the Crown, but the miners could sell it, provided they paid to the royal owners a fee, or 'royalty'. Although the free miners worked the large scale mines such as Clearwell Caves, they also had their own small private mines, which were worked by individuals or families.

Even when the National Coal Board was established, the free miners retained their rights to mine coal. Today there are three full-time free miners working in the forest, and seven part-timers. One of these owns the Hopewell Colliery, located near to Speech House, and he offers fascinating tours of the mine to the public, from Easter to October.

- Cross the stile and continue along the footpath into woods.

These woods are riddled with old mine workings, or 'scours', open cast surface workings. These are the property of the free miners, who dug long, shallow tunnels in pursuit of seams of ore. Most seams, or 'gales', were licensed to an individual miner for his own exclusive use.

- Cross another stile and continue up a dramatic path through woods, passing many more 'scours'.
- At a T-junction, turn left for 100 yards to reach the edge of the woods.
- Keep ahead over a stile and maintain your line of advance across the field to a stile beside a gate, to the right of the farm.
- Cross the stile and keep ahead along a track, a fence and hedge to your right, to cross another stile.
- Keep ahead for 20 yards, and cross a stile into a field.

- Turn immediately right along the edge of the field and follow the field boundary, turning left with the fence to go down the field to a gateway.

- Go through the gateway. IGNORE an obvious stile on the opposite side of the field but continue instead to follow the right-hand boundary of the field, keeping woods on your right hand, to reach a stile in the top right corner of the field.

- Cross the stile and go half-right, keeping the woods on your right hand. Follow the field boundary down to a gate on to a lane.

- Cross the lane and go over a stile opposite.

- Go half-right up the slope to a stile in the top right corner of the field.

- Cross the stile and go up the field, keeping the hedge close on your right.

- Go into the next field and keep ahead, the hedge still on your right, for 10 yards.

- Turn right through a gate and go along the side of the field, the hedge close on your right and a factory directly ahead.

- At a waymark post on the right, halfway along the field, turn half-left across the field, gradually converging with the factory fence and aiming for the far right-hand corner, where eventually a stile comes into sight.

- Cross the stile and continue ahead with the factory fence on your right.

- Cross a gate in the field corner and bear half-right, with hedge and trees on your right hand, to a gate to the right of a silo ahead.

- Cross a stile beside the gate and keep ahead along a track.

- At a corner bear right, ignoring a footpath going off to the left, but 10 yards later, turn left along a footpath between houses.

- Keep ahead along a road, ignoring side roads to the right, to reach a T-junction with Cinder Hill.

- Turn left down Cinder Hill for 250 yards to a mini roundabout.

On the left you pass the Forest House Hotel. Formerly known as Tump House, this was the home of David Mushet, the Scottish engineer who moved to Coleford to take over the running of the Whitcliff Foundry. His son, the pioneering Robert Forester Mushet, was born at Forest House.

- Cross the roundabout and continue down the hill for another 150 yards to reach the clock tower.

Walk 19

Bibury: the woollen industry through the ages

Distance: 4.5 miles

Map: OS 163

Start and parking: The walk starts at the Arlington Mill Museum, Bibury (grid ref: 114068). Bibury is on the A433, four miles north-east of Cirencester. There is a free car park opposite Arlington Mill (which gets crowded in summer) and roadside parking nearby.

Refreshments: Public houses, shop and seasonal tea rooms in Bibury.

Historical Background

The villages of Bibury and Ablington epitomise the progress of the cloth industry in the Cotswolds, from the early Middle Ages until the eve of the Industrial Revolution.

Throughout the Middle Ages the Cotswolds were ideal for cloth manufacture, a position unchallenged until the early 18th century. There was ample grazing for huge flocks of sheep, and an abundant supply of clear water for washing fleeces. The humid climate was ideal for working wool into yarn and weaving it into cloth. Fuller's earth, needed to treat the finished cloth, was plentiful. The teazle plant, whose spiky heads were used for raising the nap (or pile) of the cloth, were also widely available.

Commercial wool production in the Cotswolds originated in the great religious houses such as Hailes Abbey (see walk 10) and the production of cloth was initially started by merchants who diversified away from simply trading in wool into manufacture (see walk 13). Initially wool was bought in the Cotswolds and taken to nearby towns such as Bristol and Gloucester to be worked into cloth, but local landowners soon saw the potential profit to be gained by manufacturing cloth themselves from their own wool.

Cloth-making rapidly developed as a cottage industry in villages and valleys throughout the region. It was dependant upon an army of spinners and weavers, working upon spinning wheels and hand-looms in their own homes, as a supplement to any income they made from other work. Gradually some degree of mechanisation was introduced, and existing water mills were often converted to drive primitive fulling machines. Clothiers provided the capital for the purchase of wool and machinery that they supplied to landlords whose tenants worked the wool. The landlords protected their interests by making work upon their cloth a condition of tenure.

By 1600 the woollen industry was widespread across the Cotswolds, and existing market towns such as Nailsworth and Minchinhampton (see walk 3) had become wool towns. Both clothiers and workers were conservative, resisting any changes that would potential threaten their livelihood, and the industry flourished for the next two centuries. The introduction of steam power in the late 18th century led to the growth of factories centred on the Dursley-Stroud area, and the cottage industries in the Cotswolds went into terminal decline.

The Walk

This walk starts at the picturesque Arlington Row in Bibury, ascends on to the Cotswolds and follows the ancient Salt Way to the village of Ablington, with its historic tithe barn and wool mansions, before returning to Bibury.

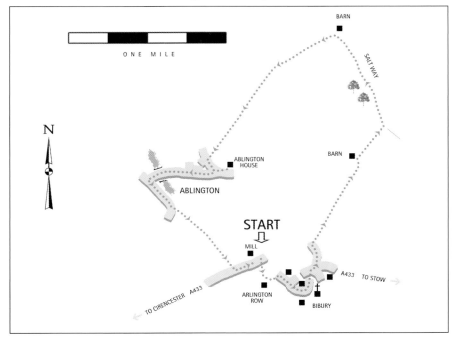

Arlington Row.

The present Arlington Mill was built in the 17th century, on the site of a much earlier mill. The Domesday Book *mentions a water-powered mill on this site, used for the grinding of corn. Many such corn mills in the Cotswolds were converted to provide power for fulling machines, giant hammers driven by water to pound the wool. Arlington Mill survived as a corn mill, but in the face of competition from new steam-powered mills in the early 19th century, it fell into disuse. It was restored in 1996 and today it is a museum of rural life.*

The mill is open mid–March to mid–November, daily, 10.30am–7pm. There is an admission charge.

- With your back to the Arlington Mill Museum, cross the road to a tarmacked footpath immediately opposite, signed 'Arlington Row'.

- Follow the footpath alongside a pleasant stream across a water meadow, called Rack Isle, to reach Arlington Row.

Arlington Row was originally built in 1380 to house the sheep owned by the monks of Osney Abbey, Oxford. The Abbey was the major feudal landlord in this area, and realised the commercial potential of wool very early. Wool was produced locally, on monastic farms, and brought to Bibury for 'fulling' i.e. degreasing. After being washed repeatedly in the nearby stream to remove all the grease, it was hung up to dry on racks on the island between the streams, soon called Rack Isle.

After the Dissolution of the Monasteries, the Abbey lands were sold to local landlords and merchants, who carried on the wool trade started by the monks. In the 17th century the sheep stalls were converted into cloth-weaving workshops, with the ground floor of each cottage being taken up entirely with a weaving frame and wool storeroom, and accommodation provided for the weaver and his family on the floor above. Each cottage was home and workshop to one family, tenants of a local wool merchant. In return for accommodation, the family were obliged to work on the wool provide by their landlord, for a piecework rate set by him. Provided the weaver worked to his landlord's satisfaction the tied cottage was passed, along with the weaving skills, from father to son.

Arlington Row was 'discovered' in the 19th century by William Morris, who perceived them as typifying the idyllic rural life he idolised. Morris declared Bibury to be the 'most picturesque village in the Cotswolds', thereby ensuring it the dubious benefit of a constant stream of tourists. Arlington Row and Rack Isle are now owned by the National Trust. The cottages are still lived in and none are open to the public.

- Pass Arlington Row and follow the footpath over a footbridge to the road.

- Turn right along the road for 100 yards, the river on your right. Where the main road bends left, keep ahead along a lane (marked with a No Entry sign).

- Follow the lane through Old Bibury, passing the church of St Mary's on your right.

The first church on this site was founded in 743 AD as a cell of St Mary's Priory, Worcester, to provide a chapel and home for a single monk. Over time a substantial church was built to serve the villagers of Bibury, initially of wood but later stone built. In 1130, after the Norman Conquest, the church became the property of Osney Abbey, Oxford, and the Saxon church was extended and adorned in the Norman style in the 13th and 14th centuries.

Some of the Saxon masonry can still be seen, especially in the chancel, below the later Norman lancet windows. The northern and particularly the southern porches are fine examples of late Norman design, as is the Norman nave, with its wooden roof.

- It is worth detouring into the tranquil rose-planted churchyard behind St Mary's, for a view of Bibury Court.

There has been a house on the site of Bibury Court since Roman times, and fragments of Roman, Saxon and Norman buildings are still to be found. Work on the present gabled building started in the Elizabethan era, but the Court was greatly extended and redeveloped in 1633 by Sir Thomas Sackville. It remained in the Sackville family for generations. In the 19th century the family engaged in a complex and protracted legal case that was the basis for Charles Dickens' Bleak House, Bibury Court being the eponymous house.

- From the church, continue to follow the lane (signed 'No Through Road') through the village. Where the lane ends, continue ahead through a wall to a junction of roads.

- Go right along the main road for a few yards. At a bend, carefully cross the road and go up a lane (signed 'No Through Road') on the left of the main road.

- Follow the lane as it winds uphill past houses. Where the lane ends at the entrance to a house, keep ahead up a grassy track to enter a field.

- Follow the track up the side of two fields, the hedge close on your right hand, climbing gently all the while.

Pause before reaching the crest of the hill to admire the fine views back over Bibury.

- Follow the track over the crest of the hill, passing a covered reservoir on your right, and continue downhill.
- Where the surfaced track turns right, keep straight on through a metal gate and follow the track down the side of a field, a wall on your left.
- Go through a metal gate and follow the track to a barn.
- Pass the barn and keep ahead along the side of the field, a wall and fence on your left, to reach a gate in the far left-hand corner of the field.
- Go through the gate and 10 yards later, turn left along a cross track.

The track you are now walking follows the route of the Salt Way, an ancient routeway that has existed since at least the early Middle Ages. Salt was a very important natural commodity until the last 200 years, with a variety of domestic uses. It was used chiefly in the preservation of foodstuffs such as meat, cheese and fish, but also used for a variety of other everyday activities, such as the preparation of clothing and the curing of toothache. The main source of salt in Britain was Droitwich in modern Worcestershire, and salt mined there was exported across the whole of the country. One of the major trade routes for this commodity was the Salt Way. Merchants would transport salt by pack mule from Droitwich, climbing on to the Cotswolds at Winchcombe (see walks 1 and 16). They then continued across the Cotswolds to Lechlade, at the head of the Thames valley, and thence down the Thames to London.

- Follow the track along the side of a field, a hedge and later woods on your left.
- Enter a second field and keep straight on, the hedge still on your left.
- Continue through a third field, the track soon partially enclosed.
- At the end of the third field, with Saltway Barn immediately ahead of you but hard to see in summer behind the hedge, turn left through a gate on the left.
- Follow the track around. In 20 yards, JUST BEFORE a gate ahead which leads to a broad track, TURN LEFT along a fainter grassy track, keeping a small building off to your left.
- In 30 yards go half-right across a concreted area to a metal gate, leading into an enclosed track.
- Follow the track out into a field and keep straight on, a fence on your right hand. Follow the track through four fields, descending slightly towards the end.
- At the end of the fourth field the track becomes enclosed. Follow the track downhill to reach a lane.

You are now entering the village of Ablington. In the Middle Ages the parish of Ablington was part of the extensive property of Osney Abbey, and the land hereabouts was devoted to rearing sheep and processing wool. Not only did the monks of Osney build Arlington Row in Bibury to store their wool, but two huge tithe barns were built here in Ablington, to store the rent the Abbey collected. The barns can be seen a little later in the walk.

- Turn left along the lane. Ignore a lane opposite leading downhill but instead follow the lane around to the left.

- In 50 yards you reach a T-junction. Continue ahead along the lane, in the direction of Bibury, for 50 yards to view the Ablington House.

Ablington House was built in the 17th century, in the gabled style that is typical of Jacobean country architecture, and which can also be seen at Bibury Court. The lions on the gateposts were brought here from the Palace of Westminster when the latter was being redeveloped.

- Return to the road junction and bear left (signed 'Winson and Fossebridge').

- Follow the road through the village of Ablington, ignoring a two side turns to the right and soon passing the Manor House behind its high walls on your left.

Ablington Manor house was built in 1590 by John Coxwell, a wealthy merchant from nearby Cirencester who had made his fortune trading in wool. At the time of the Dissolution of the Monastries, much of the land of Osney Abbey was bought up cheaply by the Coxwell family, and formed the basis of their woollen business. Five carved heads, one of Queen Elizabeth, adorn the five doorways of the house.

The Manor House was later home to the writer J. Arthur Gibbs, who in 1898 wrote A Cotswolds Village, *describing life in Ablington.*

The tithe barns built by Osney Abbey are opposite the Manor House. The barns were built to store the rent, collected in kind from the Abbey's tenants, as well as storing the produce of the Abbey's own estates. Wool was a major product to be stored here.

- Follow the road as it curves left and downhill to cross the river.

- Follow the road to a T-junction and turn left (signed 'Barnsley and Cirencester').

- In 350 yards, just after the top of the slope is reached, turn left along an enclosed footpath (signed 'Arlington') to the left of the gate to a house.

- At the end of the enclosed path, cross three stiles in quick succession, and keep ahead along the side of a field, a fence on your left.

- On the far side of the field cross two more stiles. Keep straight on across the next field, aiming to the right of a barn seen ahead.

- Pass beside the gate and cross a drive to a stile in the wall opposite.

- Pass through a band of trees and keep ahead along the side of a field, a fence on your left.

- At the end of the field, cross a stile beside a gate ahead and keep straight on along a tarmacced path, houses on your left.

- Go through a gate at the end of the path and keep ahead along a drive to reach a road.

- Turn left along the road, soon passing the Catherine Wheel public house and then the village stores. Follow the road back to Arlington Mill.

Walk 20

Dodington House, Bristol and the West Indies in the 18th century

Distance: 4 miles

Map: OS 172

Start and parking: The walk starts at the Portcullis Inn, Tormarton (grid ref: 767788). Tormarton is one mile to the north of junction 18 on the M4, approached by several minor roads off the northbound (Nailsworth) A46. The Portcullis Inn is in the middle of the village's main street, just south of the church. There is ample roadside parking in the village.

Refreshments: Public house, shop and seasonal weekend tea room in Tormarton.

Historical Background

Dodington Park was the estate of the Codington Family from 1578 until 1983, whose wealth had been built in nearby Bristol and who are typical of many of the merchant families of that city.

By 1700 Bristol was the largest port and city in England after London, and its wealth and influence derived from trade. Bristol had played a major part in colonising the New World, the departure point for explorers and later colonists throughout the 16th and 17th centuries. It was natural for Bristol to also become the leading port for trade with the New World. Bristol merchants were the first to import tobacco and sugar into England, and then worked hard to expand the demand for both. The same merchants then invested in the West Indian plantations that produced those goods, and also transported labourers from England, convicts and indented servants, to work on the plantations. When this supply of labour proved inadequate to meet the needs of the plantations, many Bristol merchants turned to the 'African Trade', the slave trade.

The trade 'Triangle' was developed: Bristol ships carried hardware and guns to Africa, which were then traded for slaves who were carried to the West Indies, there to be traded for sugar and tobacco. A handsome profit was made at each stage, and Bristol merchants grew rich on the traffic in human lives. Half of all the members of the African Company, the main slave-trading association, lived in Bristol, and for over a century, from 1660 until 1786, between 15–17,000 slaves were transported across the Atlantic each year. Usually, less than half of them survived the journey.

Some merchants were landed gentry in Gloucestershire, who had turned to trade. Others were traders and shipowners, whose increased wealth was used to buy land and status outside the confines of the city. During the 18th century many fine country houses were rebuilt or improved by Bristol merchants.

The Walk

This easy walk stays mainly on the level, and goes through and around Dodington Park, with occasional glimpses of the fine Regency house.

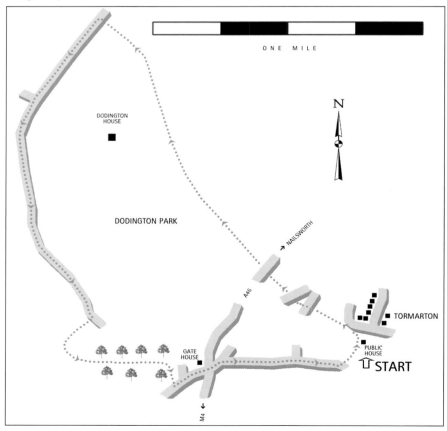

- With your back to the Portcullis Inn, turn left along the road for 100 yards.

- Where the road turns right, go left across a stone stile, signed 'Cotswolds Way'.

- Go across the field, aiming just to the left of telegraph poles, and aiming for a greenhouse to the right of a house on the opposite side of the field.

- Cross a stile in the corner of the field and descend steps into a lane.

- Cross over the lane and go up steps to cross a stile into a field.

- Keep ahead along a narrow field to another stile, leading on to a road.

- Cross the road and go quarter-left across the next field, aiming for the right-hand end of a line of tall trees ahead.

- At the end of the field, cross a stile and carefully cross the A46 to a stile opposite.

- Cross the stile and descend to cross a second stile into a field. Go half-right down the field to a stile and footbridge visible on the far side.

- Cross the footbridge and keep straight on across the next field, aiming for a stile 100 yards to the right of a metal gate and water trough visible on the opposite side.

- Cross the stile into Dodington Park.

The Codington family rose to prominence under Henry V, when John Codington was the king's standard-bearer at Harfleur and Agincourt. He was rewarded for his services with estates in Gloucestershire. The family survived the political turmoil of the next century by avoiding politics and concentrating upon their estates and a growing business in overseas

Gatehouse to Dodington Park.

trade, based upon Bristol. They became rich merchants under Henry VIII and Elizabeth, eventually buying Dodington Park, where they built an elaborate manor house as the family seat. For the next two centuries they prospered as Bristol traders, owning plantations in the West Indies and trading in sugar and tobacco.

Dodington Park was laid out in 1764 by Lancelot 'Capability' Brown, the leading landscape architect of his day. It is typical of Brown's work, with trees and green swards laid out in such a way as to emphasise the natural contours of the ground, and create an idealised landscape that was perceived as tidier and more aesthetically pleasing than nature left to its own devices.

- Maintain your line of advance along the side of the field, trees and a fence on your right hand.

- Pass a single oak and keep ahead to a stile in the far right-hand corner of the field.

- Cross the stile and maintain your line of advance, trees still on your right hand.

- Cross a stile beside a gate. DO NOT bear left down the edge of the trees but keep ahead. At the brow of the hill, bear marginally left, to descend to a single tree and through shrubs to a stile beyond.

As you descend, look left for a glimpse of Dodington House.

The present Dodington House was built on the site of the family's previous Elizabethan manor house. It was designed for Christopher Codington in 1796 by James Wyatt, who had just completed the restoration of Salisbury Cathedral. It took until 1813 for the house to be completed, but when finished, Dodington House was one of the finest Regency buildings in Gloucestershire. In design the house is almost completely square, with a huge portico on the west side, supported by six huge Corinthian columns, so widely spaced that a carriage could drive between them to the main entrance. The frontage is modelled on the Parthenon in Athens, and typifies the neo-classical architecture so loved in the regency period. Inside is a spacious marble-floored entrance hall, from which a magnificent staircase raises the full height of the building, lit by semi-circular windows set into a dome.

Wyatt barely lived to see the completion of his work, for in September 1813 he was returning from London with Christopher Codington in the latter's coach, when the coach overturned near Marlborough, killing Wyatt instantly.

- Cross the stile and go across the next field to a white marker post on the opposite side of the field.

- Cross a bridge and go through a gate.

Water features were an important part of Capability Brown's work. Dodington Park has two lakes, one higher than the other to allow for a cascade between the two. Natural streams were straightened and enclosed to make ornamental canals with ornate bridges across them. Although the stream you are crossing has been allowed to somewhat revert to nature, it still conveys the general impression Brown wished to achieve.

- Turn half-left across the field to a stile 50 yards ahead.

- Cross the driveway (the rear entrance to Dodington House) to a stile opposite. Go half-left across the next field, aiming for a metal gate on the far side.

- Cross a stile beside the gate, into a lane.

- Turn left along the lane, soon following the perimeter wall of Dodington Park.

There are good views over the wall into the grounds of Dodington House, with parkland and lawns that still largely follow the original Capability Brown design.

- Follow the lane through Home Farm, with the ornate gateway to Dodington Park between the buildings on the left.

- Follow the quiet country lane for a mile, passing a driveway to Sand Court on your right and eventually climbing on to the Cotswolds ridge.

- Follow the road between a barn on your right and a gateway (marked 'Private, please keep out') on your left. Twenty yards later, look carefully for a bridleway sign obscured by trees on your right, and turn right through scrubs into a field.

- (If you miss the sign, continue down the lane to reach the B4465 and pick up the route again.)

- Walk around the edge of the large field, keeping the hedge close on your right hand.

- At the end of the hedge, turn left and walk with a fence close on your right, to follow a footpath into woods.

- Once in the trees, the path is clearer. Follow the path through the trees to emerge on the edge of a field.

- Keep ahead along the edge of the field, in and out of the trees.

- The path re-enters the wood and descends to a fence. Turn left and walk with the fence on your right hand, to soon re-enter the trees again.

- Continue ahead on a clear path through the trees.

- At the end of the woodland path, turn right through a gap in the trees on to a path along the edge of a field.

- Keep ahead, the field on your right and houses and a road on your left, to reach the B4465.

- Turn left along the B4465, passing the junction of the lane to Dodington, keeping to the verge on the left side of the road.

Note the cottage on the right. The course of old turnpike road from Bath to Cheltenham ran beside the cottage, and along the grassy sward in front of the gates of Dodington House. The cottage was the tollbooth for the turnpike, where travellers using the privately owned and maintained road had to pay a fee for using it.

- In 100 yards you reach the A46, with the gates to Dodington House on your left.

The imposing gates to Dodington House were part of the original design. The ornate rotunda next to them, originally the gatekeepers lodge and with its echoes of a Grecian temple, is in the neo-classical design of the house itself.

Dodington House is not open to the public.

- Cross the A46 with care and go along the road opposite (signed 'Tormarton').

- In 100 yards turn right into a lane (signed 'Single Track Road').

- Keep along the lane for half a mile, ignoring a side turn to the left.

- 100 yards after passing a terrace of stone cottages on your left, and just before a bend in the road, turn left over a stile (signed 'Cotswolds Way').

- Keep ahead along a field, a wall on your right hand.

- At the end of the field keep straight on through a gap in the wall and keep ahead to a waymarked stile, beside a gate seen ahead.

- Cross the stile and keep straight on down a track to reach the lane at the Portcullis Inn.

Walk 21

Buckland Rectory: five centuries of religious change

Distance: 3 miles

Map: OS 150

Start and parking: The walk starts from the village green at Laverton (grid ref: 074356). Laverton is just to the south of the B4632 Broadway to Winchcombe road, three miles south of Broadway. There is ample roadside parking within the village, but please show consideration for residents when leaving your car.

Refreshments: None on route, although Broadway with its public houses, shops and tea rooms, is only a half-mile detour at one point.

Historical Background

The rectory at Buckland has been in continual use since it was built in 1456, and has witnessed the monumental changes that have occurred within church over the past six centuries.

At the time of the Norman Conquest Buckland was part of the Diocese of the Bishop of Worcester. After the Conquest the Saxon bishop, Wulstan, remained in office, thanks to his loyalty to King William, and although the manor of Buckland was given to Gloucester Abbey it remained part of Worcester Diocese. The first church was built in the 13th century, and for the first time Buckland got a specific parish priest. The Church owned a quarter of the land in Gloucestershire, received a tenth of all incomes of the remainder, and churchmen performed the offices of high civil servants and diplomats. Second only to the King, the Church was the greatest power in the land, was still so when Buckland rectory was first built in 1483.

Fifty years later, Henry VIII broke with the Church of Rome and much of the church's lands in England were seized by the Crown. Buckland, an insignificant parish, was unaffected. King Henry established the Church of England more for political than for theological reasons, and the content of church services, although now in English rather than Latin, was little changed. Gloucestershire largely avoided the bitter religious divisions between Protestant and Catholic that raged in neighbouring Oxfordshire throughout the Elizabethan and Stuart era, and the vicar of Buckland had no difficulty in coping with the changed order.

Buckland rectory did, however, find itself involved in the next great religious change, the growth of non-conformism in the 18th century. In 1738 John Wesley, an ordained Anglican minister, founded the Methodists, a movement which adhered strictly to religious precepts and practices and avoided the ceremony of the Anglican church. Wesley travelled extensively around the country spreading his message. The Bristol area, with its strong connection with the slave trade, was a particular target for Welsey. Few churches would allow him to preach so instead he addressed vast open air congregations. The rector of Buckland was a close friend of Wesley's, and let him use the rectory as a base for missionary journeys and as a haven for recovery from his work.

The Walk

This short walk goes through fields and woods, passing an Iron Age hill fort and Buckland Rectory. Although short, the walk is strenuous for a brief stretch, where it climbs out of Buckland to the hill fort.

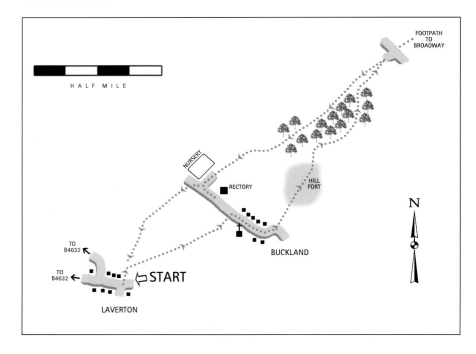

- Standing at the village green in Laverton, facing the School House, turn left at a bridleway sign beside a 'No Through Road' sign in front of you.

- Walk down the enclosed footpath, passing a telephone box.

- Where the wall on the left ends leave the enclosed footpath by a stile on the right, beside a gate.

- Go half-left across the field, passing a telegraph pole in midfield, to a stile on the far side.

- Go through a band of trees to a second stile and then keep ahead across a field, keeping a line of trees on your left hand and aiming for the tower of Buckland church seen ahead.

- Cross a stile at the end of the field and keep ahead, keeping a fence close on your left hand and following the fence as it curves right to reach another stile.

- Cross the stile and follow the enclosed footpath.

- At the end of the path turn left over a stile and immediately turn right, resuming your former direction, the fence still on your right hand. Follow the fence to a squeeze stile and out on to a road.

- Turn right and follow the road through Buckland, to reach St Michael's Church on your right.

The manor of Buckland was the property of Gloucester Abbey from 709 AD. It was a small agricultural community that was not large enough to justify its own church until the 13th century, when St Michael's was built. The church was restored three times, on each occasion additions being made, and in consequence it now displays work from every main architectural period since its foundation to the present day. The tower was built in the 14th century and its grotesque gargoyles added the next century. The nave was heightened in the 15th century and a clerestory added. At the same time it was given a splendid king-post roof, which has been repainted in the original colours. There are pews from the 15th century, high-backed stalls dated 1615 and a 17th century pulpit. The stained glass east window, donated by William Grafton, the rector here between 1466 and 1510, was restored by William Morris in 1883.

In the churchyard is a Celtic cross, itself dating from the 19th century but being a faithful replica of a 14th-century cross, which stood on the same spot. The plinth is original. The Celtic cross is a reflection of the influence of the Celtic rather than the Roman church on the spread of Christianity in this area (see walk 6).

- Follow the road as it curves left, climbing steadily through the village. Continue up the road, eventually marked as 'No Through Road'.

- Where the road curves to the right in front of Hillside Cottage, go half-left, passing to the immediate left of Hillside Cottage and the adjoining Bothy, to enter an enclosed footpath.

- Follow the path up to a stile. Cross the stile and keep ahead to climb steep wooden steps on to Burhill hill fort.

You are now entering the Iron Age hill fort of Burhill. The fort, which was not discovered until 1960, was only small, a matter of only a few acres. It was built by cutting off the neck of a spur with a ditch and rampart, and then fortifying the other three, steep sides with an additional earthen rampart, which on top of the steep slopes you have just climbed would have made the fort very hard to attack. It is unlikely that Burhill was regularly garrisoned: it is most likely that it served to provide shelter in times of emergency to the isolated farms in the valley beneath.

- At the top of the steps keep ahead up the steep slope. Soon a faint path leads to a waymark post and then to a stile on the skyline.

- Cross the stile and maintain your line of advance to a waymark post seen ahead, and then to the corner of a fence directly ahead.

Broadway Tower is visible to your right, a landmark dominating the Cotswolds skyline in this area. The tower has no historic significance: it was built in 1800 by the Earl of Coventry as a gothic folly to enhance the view from his nearby home of Croome Court.

- Keep ahead, the fence on your left, to a gate.

You are now going through the rampart and ditch built across the neck of a spur to defend the fort on this, its weakest side. The fort itself covered the area of the field behind you, which would have been a large open area for sheltering goats, sheep and cattle, with room for temporary shelters for the population fleeing from their more substantial homes in the valley bottom.

- Go through the gate and turn left along the boundary of the next field, the fence on your left hand.

- Follow the fence as it bears right, eventually reaching a stile and gate in the field corner.

- Go through the gate and turn right to follow a path down through trees, staying on the waymarked path and ignoring side turns.

- Leave the wood through a gate and continue down the side of the field, trees on your left.

- Follow the left-hand hedge down to a stile leading into an enclosed footpath.

- Follow the footpath to a stile on to a road. Once over the stile, immediately turn sharp left over a second stile, and walk up a tarmacked drive for 15 yards to another stile.

- (If you wish to detour into Broadway for refreshments, go out on to the road and follow a footpath immediately opposite, which leads in a quarter of a mile to the outskirts of Broadway. A left turn then brings you into the town centre.)

Buckland Rectory.

- Cross the stile and keep ahead up the field to a stile leading into the woods ahead.

- Follow the path through the fringe of the woods for half a mile. Stay on the level and ignore all paths leading uphill, deeper into the woods.

- At the end of the wood, cross a stile by a gate and turn right. Follow a faint track around the side of the hill, passing more trees close on your left hand.

- At a broken down stile, where waymarks give a choice of routes, TURN RIGHT. With your back to the trees, bear left and downhill on a waymarked path around the hillside, the roofs of huge greenhouses soon coming into view.

- Follow the path, soon with a fence on your right, to a stile by a field gate. Continue top follow the right-hand fence to a second stile.

- Keep ahead for 20 yards to a third stile and keep ahead down an enclosed track to a pedestrian gate leading out to the head of a lane.

- Follow the lane out to a road.

- Turn left for 50 yards to see the Old Rectory.

William Grafton, rector of St Michael's from 1466 to 1510, built the rectory as his residence, extending an existing small house between 1466 and 1483 to create a more spacious home. It still has a fine open Great Hall with an impressive hammer-beam roof and medieval stained-glass windows. The building was much altered in Victorian times. It is the oldest medieval parsonage still in use in Gloucestershire. Note the Celtic cross on the gable end.

In the early 18th century the Reverend Lionel Kirkham was rector of Buckland, living in the rectory with his large family. John Wesley was a close friend of all the Markham family, and often stayed in Buckland rectory in the years before his departure to America in 1735. At Oxford Wesley had been deeply influenced by the views of George Whitfield (see walk 3) and upon his return founded the Methodist movement. Wesley lived and worked in Oxford, but frequently travelled into Gloucestershire to preach. Bristol in particular was the target of his attentions, for he viewed the slave trade as particularly abhorrent. Wesley continued to visit Buckland at intervals, where he found the peace and tranquillity a welcome respite from his often frenetic life. Wesley, however, was an indefatigable worker, often unable to resist working even when on holiday, and used Buckland as a base from which to tour the vicinity and preach. He preached a well-advertised sermon to a packed church in nearby Stanton in 1733 (see walk 24). Wesley did not, however, preach in Buckland itself, perhaps in deference to his Anglican host.

Buckland Rectory is occasionally open to the public in the summer.

- After seeing the rectory, retrace your steps to the lane you came out of. Continue along the main road, passing a telephone box and the entrance to nurseries.

- 50 yards past the telephone box, bear left off the road into a bridleway, beside the gates of a house on the opposite side of the road.

- Follow the enclosed bridleway into a field, where it continues as a surfaced path.

- The bridleway soon becomes enclosed again. Follow the enclosed path back to the village green at Laverton.

Walk 22

Sapperton Tunnel: canal mania in the 18th century

Distance: 6 miles

Map: OS 163

Start and parking: The walk starts from the church in Oakridge Lynch, referred to on the OS map merely as 'Oakridge' (grid ref: 913033). Oakridge is six miles east of Stroud in a network of small roads just north of the A419 Stroud to Cirencester road, but the easiest approach is from the direction of Bisley. Follow signs for Oakridge Lynch. There is ample roadside parking around the village green and approach roads, but please park with consideration for residents.

Refreshments: Public house and shop in Oakridge Lynch, public house at Daneway.

Historical Background

In 1761 a revolution in transport occurred, when Francis Egerton, 2nd Duke of Bridgewater threw his energies into constructing a canal to connect his coalmines in Worsley to nearby Manchester, and opened the first commercial canal in England. The potential for canals as a means of economically moving heavy goods quickly and cheaply was immediately recognised, and during the next 60 years canals were constructed piecemeal the length and breadth of Britain. For each canal to be built a joint stock company had to be created to raise the finance, with the return on the investment coming from its commercial operation. Such was the glamour of this latest technology that private investors flocked to the canal companies, with little thought that canals were not guaranteed money-makers.

With the onset of the industrial revolution, existing road and river routes were unable to cater for the long-distance haulage of goods, especially eastwards. Canals were seen as the way to create a link between the Severn and the Thames, and thus connect Bristol and the industrial areas of Gloucestershire with London. In 1782 Robert Wentworth surveyed the route for a 29-mile long canal, which he estimated would cost £128,000. The chief engineering problem was a tunnel at Sapperton, the cost of which Wentworth refused to estimate. Despite this omission, such was the mania for investing in canals that money for the venture was rapidly raised.

The Thames & Severn Canal was opened in 1789, and from the outset it was not a success. Trade was primarily one-way, west to east, and thus the revenue generated by the canal never came close to reaching the optimistic forecasts. Leaks in the canal led to water levels falling so low in the summers that the canal had to be closed. The Sapperton Tunnel leaked badly, and its maintenance was an ongoing heavy cost. In 1810 the Kennet & Avon Canal was opened, providing a more direct link between London and the Severn and Bristol, and although the Thames & Severn Canal continued to operate, it was effectively finished as a commercial venture. Like many companies formed when 'canal mania' was sweeping Britain, the Thames & Severn Canal Co never recouped its original investment, leaving many private investors bewildered and ruined, the unfortunate result of their own naivety.

The Walk

This walk is reasonably long but not demanding. It follows the course of the old Thames & Severn Canal for its outward leg, and then makes a short steep ascent through woods before a gentle return across fields and occasional country lanes.

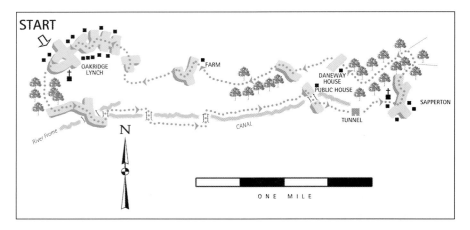

- Standing facing the village green in Oakridge Lynch, walk passing the school on your right and the church of St Bartholemew's on your left. At the end of the green keep ahead, passing between Stokes Close on the right and Fairview on the left, to a squeeze stile beside a gate.

- Cross the stile and walk with the building on your left for 20 yards to cross a stile beside a gate.

- Walk down the field, the hedge on your left, to cross a stile beside a gate in the bottom left-hand corner.

- Keep ahead for 10 yards across this narrow field to go over another stile.
- Turn right down the next field, keeping the hedge on your left, to reach a stile at the bottom of the field, leading into woods.
- Cross the stile and descend steeply, a fence on your left hand, to another stile in 30 yards.
- Cross this stile and follow a path down through the woods, passing a Gloucester Wildlife Trust sign.
- At a T-junction of paths bear left and continue down through woods to reach a terraced lane.
- Turn left along the lane for 400 yards to a T-junction.
- Turn right, signed 'Frampton Mansell', crossing the River Frome by a road bridge.
- Turn left with the road for 20 yards and then turn left down steps and over a footbridge.
- Turn right along the path.

This path follows the tow path of the Thames & Severn Canal, with the canal on your right and the River Frome on your left.

Thames & Severn Canal was opened in 1789, when the completion of the Sapperton Tunnel provided the last link in its course. It linked the River Thames with the Stroudwater Canal and thus with the Severn, providing a cross-country link in the canal network. Initially the canal was extremely busy, carrying iron and coal from the Forest of Dean, and

The entrance to Sapperton Tunnel.

wool and cloth from the South Cotswolds wool towns, to markets in the Midlands and London. Trade was however primarily one-way: in a typical year 34,000 tons of goods being carried eastwards, and only 3,000 tons travelling westwards. The high cost of maintaining the canal, especially the Sapperton Tunnel, meant that it was never a commercial success. It ceased to be used for traffic in 1911, and in 1927 all maintenance ceased and it was finally abandoned.

As you walk along the tow path a viaduct soon becomes visible. This was built in 1841 to carry the Great Western Railway. Progressive developments in transport can be seen, as road, canal, and railway all follow the same course through the Frome valley.

- In 600 yards notice a disused lock on your right, and shortly after, go through a kissing gate and turn right across a bridge over the canal.

- Turn left and walk along a track, a former lock on your left, for 30 yards, then leave the track by continuing ahead through a kissing gate. Continue on a footpath along the side of the canal.

- Continue along the towpath for nearly a mile, the canal on your left and the River Frome on your right. After half a mile you will pass under a brick bridge and continue ahead.

- At the end of the mile, cross a wooden bridge on your left and then turn right to continue along the towpath, the canal now on your right.

- Climb past a flight of disused locks, to reach a road opposite the Daneway Inn.

The Daneway Inn was built in the 18th century, initially to provide for the needs of the 'Navigators' who built the canal. These navigators, or 'navvies', were large gangs of labourers, who moved around the country following work, digging out the canals by hand, with pick, shovel and wheelbarrow. Not only did they dig the canals and locks, but also the tunnels such as the nearby Sapperton Tunnel. Gangs of miners worked around the clock, seven days a week, to blast and dig the tunnel through the hillside. Later the inn served the bargees and 'leggers' who worked on the completed canal.

- Turn right over the road bridge and then immediately turn left through a squeeze stile beside a metal gate, on to a footpath.

- Continue along the footpath, still former towpath.

The canal ran under what is now the pub car park.

- In half a mile reach the entrance to Sapperton Tunnel.

The Sapperton Tunnel was built between 1784 and 1789, the final link in the Thames & Severn Canal. At 3,400 yards long, it was the longest tunnel in Britain when it opened, and is still the third longest transport tunnel in England. The height of the ridge here meant that it was not practical to carry the canal over the top by locks, but instead it had to be tunnelled through the hillside.

There is no towpath through the tunnel and transit was via 'leggers', freelance workers who used to walk barges through the tunnel by lying on their backs and pushing against the walls and ceiling with their feet.

The opening of the tunnel, in the year of the French Revolution, was praised in the Times *as a symbol of England's stability. Soon, however, the cost of maintaining the tunnel became a serious burden on the canal management. Water leaked continually through the porous limestone of the tunnel and rock falls were common. It was the ongoing cost of maintaining the Sapperton Tunnel that finally led to the canal being abandoned as economically unviable. In 1876 it was bought by the Great Western Railway company, whose line runs parallel to the canal, and who wished to prevent any rival railway company building a track along the canal's course. The GWR never seriously tried to operate the canal as a commercial venture, preferring instead to put freight on to their railway. The canal was allowed to decline and was finally shut down in 1911.*

The other end of the tunnel, at the Tunnel House Inn, was restored in 1977, and there were plans to open the full length of the tunnel again, as a public footpath. However, it has been discovered that thousands of bats have now colonised the tunnel, and as they are a protected species whose habitat cannot be disturbed, these plans are currently shelved.

- Go up the path to the top of the tunnel. Turn left across the parapet and up steps to a stile.

- Cross the stile and go half-right up the field, aiming to the right of Sapperton Church visible on the skyline.

As you climb the steep hillside, it can be readily appreciated why a tunnel rather than locks was chosen to get the canal across this ridge.

- Cross a stile at the top of the slope and turn left along an enclosed footpath.

- Follow the footpath to a lane and turn left. At a T-junction in front of the churchyard turn right and follow the footpath uphill to the road at Sapperton.

The church is dedicated to St Kenelm, whose shrine is at Winchcombe Abbey (see walks 1 and 16). It is Norman in origin but the present structure is mainly from 1702, when the church was rebuilt.

Some cottages in the village date from the 17th century, whilst others were built by members of the Sapperton Group, an arts and crafts movement that existed in the decade before World War One. The Group was founded by Ernest Barnsley, his brother Sidney, and his business partner Ernest Gimson, and was heavily influenced by the ideas of William Morris. Using nearby Daneway House as a base, they produced extremely fine furniture, and also built several houses and the village hall here in Sapperton. The three founder members of the group are buried in St Kenelm's.

- Turn left and go down the road (signed 'No Through Road'), turning left with the road in 150 yards and continuing downhill past a turreted house.

- Ignore footpaths on your left and continue down the lane. Where the lane ends at a gate into a house, turn left down a footpath.

- Follow the footpath across a stream, and then follow the path uphill into woods.
- In 150 yards ignore a footpath going sharp left back on yourself, but continue along the main path, now flattening out, for 30 yards to reach a fork.
- Fork left uphill, soon climbing steeply.
- At a cross-track near the top of the slope, turn left. Follow the track for half a mile as it undulates around the side of the hill.
- Ignore turns to the right and continue, soon downhill, to reach a kissing gate into a road.

As you descend look left to glimpse Daneway House, which dates from 14th century with 17th century additions. In the years leading up the World War One, it was home to the Sapperton Group. The house contains the Group's furniture workshops and showrooms.

Daneway House can be viewed by appointment only, March–October. Admission charge.

- Turn left down the road for 10 yards and then turn right over a stile.
- Take the left-hand gate (NOT the gateway into an enclosed track) and follow the path around the side of the hill.
- Continue ahead along a broad grassy sward, a fence on your right and trees and bushes off to your left. At the end of this open sward, cross a stile into a lane.
- Turn right up the lane. Follow the lane for 200 yards, over the crest of the hill and down again, and then turn left over a stile by the gate to Spring Bank House.
- Go along the drive, Ignore a stile to the left in 20 yards, but continue along the drive for a further 50 yards. Just before the house, turn left through a gap in the hedge and follow a footpath along the top of a gully.
- Follow the path as it descends through trees to reach a stile on the left.
- Cross the stile and keep ahead for 20 yards to go over a footbridge.
- Keep ahead across the next field and over a fence into woods.
- Follow the path uphill through trees to a gate into a field.
- Go half-right across the field to a gate, in a direct line to the farm seen ahead.
- Go through this gate and maintain your line of advance, aiming to the left of the farm buildings.
- Pass the barn close on your right hand to reach a metal gate leading into an enclosed footpath.
- Follow the footpath out to a lane and turn left down the lane.
- Ignore a left turn in 200 yards but keep ahead along the lane.
- 50 yards later, where the lane turns right, keep ahead through a gate into a field.

- Keep ahead along the field, the fence on your left hand.

- Cross a stile and maintain your line of advance across the next field, aiming for a telegraph pole in midfield and avoiding losing height. Pass the telegraph pole and continue ahead to a stile by a gate in the top corner of the field.

- Cross the stile and go half-right across the corner of the next field, to a stile 50 yards up from the field corner. Cross this stile and turn left up a lane, the field on your left and houses on your right.

- At a T-junction at the top of the lane, cross over the road to go through a squeeze stile.

- Go half-left across a recreation field to a gate in the far left-hand corner.

- Go half-right across the lane and into a side road opposite.

- Follow the side road. Keep straight on at a crossroads, a chapel on your left.

- After 100 yards, bend right uphill with the road, and immediately around the bend turn left into a side road.

- Continue along this road, soon passing the village shop, and follow the road out to a T-junction.

- If you wish to visit The Butchers Arms public house, turn right for 200 yards. otherwise turn left and follow the road over a crossroads and back to the village green.

Walk 23

Daylesford: Warren Hastings and the foundation of the British Empire

Distance: 5 miles

Map: OS 163

Start and parking: The walk starts from the village hall in Adlestrop (grid ref: 243272). Adlestrop is on a minor road one mile north of the A436, three miles east of Stow-on-the-Wold. There is a car park in front of the village hall that is free, although a voluntary contribution would be appreciated.

Refreshments: Shop in Adlestrop, public house and shop in Oddington.

Historical Background

Warren Hastings was born in 1732 in Churchill, the next village to Daylesford. The happiest days of his early childhood was spent in Daylesford, where his grandfather was rector and owner of the manor, but the family were forced by debt to sell the estate. Hastings was sent to London to be educated into a mercantile career, and in 1750 he joined the East India Company and sailed to India, where he stayed for the next 14 years, steadily rising through the company's ranks.

The East India Company was steadily becoming the effective ruler of India, a sub-continent divided into numerous small principalities, whose trade, finances and laws were increasingly dictated by the company. Amongst both British officials and local rulers and merchants, corruption and inefficiency were rife. In 1773 the company decided to reform its operations, appointing Hastings as Governor-General of Bengal to do this. He set about reforming the fiscal and judicial systems, removing corrupt officials, withdrawing monopolies, and sidelining unreliable local rulers. He used the company's private army to extend the company's power in a series of short, sharp military ventures. In all this Hastings met with strong resistance from vested interests amongst both local landowners and company officials, and many unsuccessful attempts were made to remove him from office.

In 1785, his work done, Hastings returned to England with a modest fortune, the fruits of 35 years service and savings, and re-bought the family estates of Daylesford, which he set about restoring. However, liberal opinion in England increasingly opposed the way the company exploited its 'subjects' and looked for a scapegoat. In 1786 Hastings was impeached before the House of Lords for corruption. The trial, which began in 1788, dragged on for seven years, bankrupting Hastings. In 1814 Hastings was publically vindicated when he was made a Privy Councillor to George III. His health failing, Hastings retired to Daylesford, and died there in 1818.

Warren Hastings has pursued the interests of the East India Company honestly and forcefully, and in the process laid the foundations for the British Empire in India. A 'maverick' with unequalled executive ability, he was not a scrupulous politician, often believing that the ends justified the means. Unfortunately for Hastings, by the end of the 18th century England was awakening to a sense of its duty to humanity rather than narrow commercial interests, and Hastings was condemned for being too much of the old school.

The Walk

This walk starts in the village of Adlestrop and goes through Daylesford Estate, former home of Warren Hastings. It then

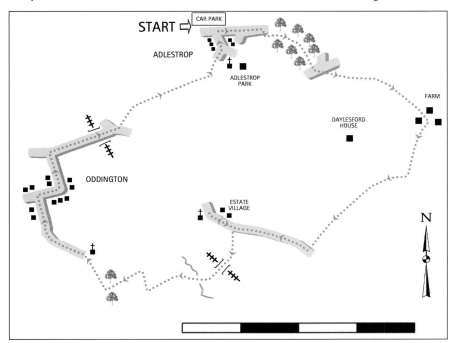

passes Hastings' tomb at Daylesford Church, goes on to Oddington Church and returns across Adlestrop Park.

- Turn left out of the village hall car park, passing a road on your right with a shelter and 'Adlestrop railway' sign.

The sign and bench is all that remains of Adlestrop railway station, closed under the Beeching cuts.

- Continue along the lane, ignoring another road to the right in 200 yards.

- 60 yards before the lane bends to the right, at the top of a rise, look for a footpath sign and stile on your right.

- Cross the stile and turn left to walk through trees.

- Ignore a gate into a field on your right but continue ahead through the trees.

- Climb gently with the path, over a cross track. Keep ahead, the path now flatter, to reach a stile beside a gate leading on to the A436.

- Turn left and walk along the grass verge for 30 yards, to where the lane from Adlestrop joins the main road.

- Cross the main road to the gates of West Lodge and continue along the main road for another 10 yards, then turn right through a wooden gate, at a footpath sign.

You are now in the grounds of Daylesford Estate.

- Keep ahead along a path through trees to reach a paddock fence.

- Turn left and walk with the fence on your right hand. Where the fence turns right around the perimeter of the first paddock, cross a stile ahead.

- Maintain your line of advance across the middle of a second paddock, to a gate on the far side.

- Go through the gate and turn right between paddocks for 15 yards, and then turn left along an enclosed path (a third paddock is now on your left).

- Continue ahead past a fourth paddock and over a stone bridge.

- Continue ahead along a broad, tree-lined drive.

This ornamental drive is one of many such that connects the various parts of the Daylesford Estate. It was laid down between 1787-93, when the estate was formally landscaped.

- At a cross track, keep ahead along a surfaced drive, towards buildings.

- Cross a stile and keep ahead through the farmyard (now mainly housing and enterprise zone, although with a working horse-breeding farm attached).

- At the end of the farmyard, in front of Hill Farm Cottage, turn right, signed 'To gardens'.

- Keep ahead along a broad surfaced drive, at first with paddocks on your right hand and then with the high wall of the Daylesford Estate.

- Pass gates and keep straight on. In 200 yards ignore a turn to the left but turn right along the main drive, the wall still on your right. The wall eventually gives way to hedgerow.

- Follow the drive past parkland to the road.

The formal ornamental parkland surrounding Daylesford House was laid out in 1787, by landscape gardener Humphrey Repton. It followed the fashion of the time established by Lancelot 'Capability' Brown, for creating a tidy view of nature. The stands of woods followed the contours of the land, and were also positioned to hide the house from prying eyes.

- Turn right along the lane for half a mile, Daylesford Park on the right, to reach the gates to the park and the estate houses on the right.

In winter, when the trees are bare, it is just possible to glimpse Daylesford House. Warren Hastings had always dreamed of buying back the family estate, and in 1787 he did. He set about building a fine mansion, designed by Samuel Cockerell, the architect employed by the East India Company and thus a business colleague as well as a friend of Hastings. Daylesford is almost entirely classical in design, with a central Moorish dome. Hastings had not anticipated the crippling cost of defending himself in the House of Lords, and work upon Daylesford frequently foundered, during which time Cockerell worked upon designing nearby Sezincote House.

The village at the entrance of the grounds was built to house the workers upon the estate. It was designed as a whole, so that the cottages blended with one another and also with the landscape. Daylesford, as well as having a formal park, was a working estate and a highly-profitable one.

Daylesford House is not open to the public.

- Opposite the drive to the estate, turn left along a bushy path to St Peter's Church.

The original Saxon and Norman church, falling into disrepair and actually unsafe, was taken down by Warren Hastings in 1816, who in the last two years of his life rebuilt it largely as it had been previously. It was primarily designed to serve the tenants of the Daylesford Estate, and contained a 'squires box' for the use of the Hastings family. By 1860 however, the church was too small for the growing population of the parish and it was radically redesigned and extended. The building was paid for by Harman Grisewood, the then owner of Daylesford, who employed architect J.L. Pearson to rebuild the church in an ornately 'French Gothic' style.

Inside the church are monuments to Warren Hastings and his wife, and a brass to William Gardiner, whose daughter married into the Hastings family and was the founder of the family fortune. Outside the east window of the church is the tomb of Warren Hastings, surmounted by a simple Grecian urn.

- Return to the road and turn right. Retrace your steps for 100 yards, and then turn right at a footpath sign, over a stile beside a metal field gate.

- Walk along the side of the field, the hedge on your right hand, to a railway bridge in the far corner.

- Cross the bridge and follow the track for 100 yards into a field.

- Go half-right across the field to a pedestrian gate leading on to a footbridge.

- Cross the footbridge and turn right. Follow the field boundary around the edge of the field, turning left soon.

- Continue ahead along a grassy track along the side of the field, the hedge on your right hand.

- At the end of the field, follow the track around two sides of the next field, first turning right and then left in the field corner, keeping the boundary hedge on your right hand.

- In the far right corner of the field, follow the track right through a band of trees to a T-junction of tracks.

Tomb of Warren Hastings, Daylesford church.

- Turn right and follow the track to the head of a lane at Oddington Church.

St Nicholas' Church, Oddington, was more or less abandoned in 1862, when a new church was built in the village. The church was early Norman, but substantially altered in the 13th century by the Archbishop of York, who had a residence at Oddington and needed a church fit for royal visits. A new nave and chancel were added to the original Norman nave, giving impressive dimensions. Well worth seeing is a well preserved 14th-century wall painting depicting the Last Judgement.

- Continue along the lane into the village of Oddington.

- At a T-junction, turn right and follow the road through the village. Turn left with the road past the public house on your left and Oddington House on your right.

- Follow the road out to a junction with the A436.

- Turn right along the main road. Use the pavement on the right hand to start with, and where it ends, cross the road and use the left-hand pavement to go over a railway bridge. (DO NOT be tempted on to a private road to the left at this point.)

- 80 yards after the bridge, turn left into a side road to Adlestrop, and 20 yards later, turn right over a stile.

- Cross a second stile into Adlestrop Park and keep ahead, aiming directly at the large building of Adlestrop Park ahead.

The mansion of Adlestrop Park dates from the 16th century, but the Gothic south-west front that faces you was added in the 18th century, when the park was formally laid out. This Gothic house provided Jane Austin, who often visited the nearby rectory, with the model for Northanger Abbey.

- Join a grassy cross-track just before the cricket pitch and turn left to follow the track around the perimeter of the cricket green to a waymarked pedestrian gate, beside a field gate. (DO NOT veer right on to the obvious path leading towards the school.)

- Go through the gate and continue along the enclosed grassy track. Pass through a gateway and follow the track out to a lane.

Adlestrop House, on the left, was formerly the rectory and the home to the Revd Theophilus Leigh. Leigh was Master of Balliol College, Oxford, and his family owned the nearby Adlestrop Park. His niece was Jane Austin, who often visited Adlestrop House.

The church of St Mary Magdalene on the right contains many memorials to members of the Leigh family, who lived in Adlestrop Park from 1553.

- Follow the lane past the church and bear left.

- At a T-junction, go left past the post office and down the village street.

- Follow the lane out to a T-junction, with the village hall car park half-left in front of you.

Walk 24

Snowshill, Stanton and rural decline in the 19th century

Distance: 6 miles

Map: OS 150

Start and parking: The walk starts at the free car park (grid ref: 097340) in the village of Snowshill, which is in a network of minor roads three miles south of Broadway. Snowshill is best approached from Broadway, and the car park is on the outskirts of the village as you approach.

Refreshments: Public houses in Snowshill and Stanton.

Historical Background

The villages of Snowshill and Stanton were part of the vast estates of Winchcombe Abbey until the Dissolution of the Monasteries, when they were sold to private landlords. The days of feudal obligations on the part of both landowner and tenant were past, and the new landlords were keenly interested in maximising the profits from their lands. The Cotswolds were an unattractive farming region, with thin, stony soil, and sheep remained the major source of income until the end of the 18th century.

Nevertheless, the end of feudalism enabled landowners to innovate. In medieval times villages were surrounded by two or sometimes three huge, open fields, with each villager, including the landlord, owning a number of strips of land within each field. Every operation had to be conducted in common, and no one could produce crops at a different time or that required different treatment to his neighbours. Once feudal obligations were dispensed with, the land tenure of villagers was increasingly converted to short-term or flexible leaseholds, and as the lease came up the open fields was enclosed by the landlord. Even more unpopular, common land, which had been a source of free grazing and winter foodstuff, was also enclosed. Individual villagers who had lived by subsistence farming on their small holdings, increasingly became paid labourers on someone else's land, and by the start of the 18th century the small farmer had all but disappeared. At the same time, increased mechanisation reduced the amount of labouring work needed.

Farming in England went into recession in the 19th century, in the face of cheap food imported from America and Australia. A series of disastrous harvests in the last quarter of the century drove many communities into abject poverty. The only escape was to move to the nearby industrial towns to seek work in the textile and other industries. Traditional villages like Snowshill and Stanton, their communities dispersed, fell into disrepair. Both were lucky to be rescued by enlightened landlords: many other Cotswolds farming communities were not so fortunate.

The Walk

This walk starts in the village of Snowshill and crosses fields to descend the Cotswolds, one of the most spectacular parts of the ridge. It goes on to Stanton and then climbs back up the Cotswolds to Snowshill.

● To visit Snowshill Manor, turn left along the lane for a hundred yards, or alternatively, follow the signed footpath out of the car park.

The village of Snowshill, together with nearby Stanton (visited later on the walk), was the

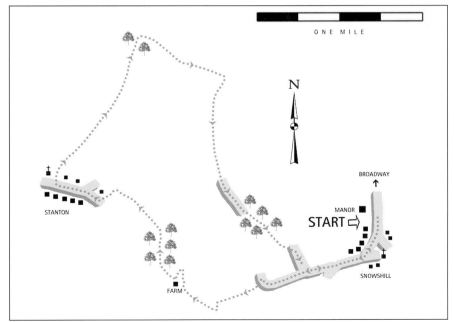

feudal property of Winchcombe Abbey. A large percentage of the community's produce was paid to the Abbey in tithes, and a small manor was built in the village to administer their collection. After the Dissolution of Winchombe Abbey in 1539, its estates were sold piecemeal into private hands. Snowshill was briefly retained by King Henry VIII, and then given to his sixth queen, Catherine Parr (see also walk 16). The existing manor, built around 1500, was converted into a substantial half-timbered farmhouse, and used as the administrative centre of the estate, which remained in the Parr family for several generations. In the late 17th century a splendid William & Mary south front was added.

In 1919 Snowshill was bought by Charles Wade, whose family were Bristol merchants who had amassed a fortune from sugar plantations in the West Indies (see also walk 20). Wade restored the house himself, using period tools to carve oak panelling in the Tudor style. He also cleared the grounds of a number of Victorian outhouses and laid out formal gardens, based upon a series of small and diverse enclosures. As a gentleman of leisure Wade was free to pursue his artistic and scholarly interests, and travelled extensively, collecting items that took his interest. Consequently, Snowshill houses an extraordinary range of objects, from Japanese armour to Victorian chamber pots.

Wade retired to the West Indies in 1951 and gave Snowshill Manor to the National Trust.

Snowshill Manor is open 1 April–30 October, 1pm–5pm, closed on Tuesdays. Admission charge, free to National Trust members.

- For the walk, leave the car park and turn right along the lane. Follow the lane through the village of Snowshill, passing the Snowshill Arms on the right and the church on the left.

The church of St Barnabas was largely rebuilt in 1864, although its earlier Perpendicular tower still survives.

- Follow the lane out of the village. Ignore a footpath on the right but follow the lane as it climbs out of the village.

- Just before the top of the hill, turn right down a lane (signed 'No Through Road').

- In 300 yards, ignore a turn to the left but continue along the lane, soon also ignoring a footpath off to the left.

- Where the lane bends sharp right at the top of a hill, turn left through a waymarked gate.

- Go half-right across the corner of a field, aiming for a footpath post seen at the hedge on the skyline.

- Go through a pedestrian gate beside the footpath post and maintain the same line of advance across the next field. Once over the brow of the field a post comes into sight in the far corner of the field.

- Pass the post and turn left into an enclosed track.

- In 40 yards, TURN RIGHT through double metal gates and follow a track along the side of the field, the hedge on your left hand (a breeze-block building in mid field will denote that you are in the right field).

- Follow the track to a farm. Turn right along the side of the barn and in 15 yards turn left between barns to a gate.

- Follow the farm track as it bears right and leaves the farm. Follow the track to a gate.

- At a T-junction just beyond the gate, turn left along a track (signed 'Stanton').

The rolling dip slope of the Cotswolds, sloping gently away on your right, was in the sixth century the territory of the Saxon chieftain 'Cud' or 'Cod'. The Saxon word for this type of gently sloping high pasture was 'wold', and hence this area became known as 'Cod's wold'. Eventually the name became associated with the whole of the limestone ridge from Bath to Chipping Campden.

- DO NOT follow the track through the gates to a house but instead go through a gate to their right.

- Follow a clear footpath as it sweeps around the sides of two dry valleys, veering firstly sharp right and then even sharper left, descending all the time.

The curious mounds around the hillside you are walking on are the double rampart of Shenbarrow Camp, an Iron Age hill fort. The 2½ acre site was first excavated in 1935, and evidence was discovered that the fort had been occupied for at least some of its history. It is probable that it was first built as an emergency shelter for the local farmers in time of trouble, like nearby Beckbury Camp (see walk 9) but later some families at least moved into the fort as a semi-permanent dwelling place.

- Soon magnificent views open up across the Isbourne valley, with Bredon Hill beyond and Stanton nestling in the valley.

- Follow the path through a gate and down through woods.

- At a T-junction, after the path has passed through gateposts, turn left and follow the track, soon curving around the open hillside.

- Cross an enclosed track and keep ahead along the clear path, ignoring side turns.

- Follow the track as it bends left with the field boundary and descends, soon curving right again into the valley bottom.

- Pass through a gate and continue along the broad track, in a few yards ignoring a footpath to the left (the Cotswolds Way).

- Follow the track through gates and into the outskirts of the village of Stanton. The track soon becomes tarmacKed and passes Little Sheppey House on the left. Continue down the lane to join the village street.

- Turn left and walk through the village to reach the market cross.

In feudal times, the village of Stanton was owned by Winchcombe Abbey, a community based upon the herding of sheep and the tilling of the land. The first village was timber-built, and lay in the shelter of the Cotswolds scarp, where wood was plentiful. By the 16th century, it was becoming common to build even lowly cottages out of stone, in Stanton's case locally excavated oolite. Many of the houses in the main street date from that time. Along with many Cotswolds villages, Stanton suffered during the agricultural depression that lasted for much of the later 19th century. Poverty and migration of workers, either into the cities or abroad, left the village half empty and its buildings dilapidated. In 1906 the architect Sir Philip Stott bought Stanton Court, and became squire of the village. He not only restored the Court but also set about restoring many of the houses in the village. The beautiful main street of the village down which you are walking, lined with fine stone cottages that typify the Cotswolds, owes its appearance and preservation to Stott.

- Immediately before the cross turn right along a lane to the gates of the manor house.

The present building is 16th century, on the site of an earlier manor house, placed conveniently adjacent to the church. The manor never fell into the same disrepair as many properties in the village, and did not need Sir Philip's restoration work. Consequently it is rather overshadowed by Sir Philip's home, Stanton Court, at the other end of the village.

- Turn left through the gate into the churchyard.

The church of St Michael's is late Norman, with the spire, tower and two-storey crenellated

Village of Stanton.

porch added during the Perpendicular period. Unusually it contains two pulpits, a disused 14th-century one and a later one from the Jacobean period. Sir Philip Stott commissioned the eminent architect Sir Ninian Comper to restore the church, removing some Victorian additions and adding his own west gallery and rood, very much in keeping with the Norman original. Comper used stained glass from Hailes Abbey in the east window, incorporating it into a design of his own which includes his personal trademark, the wild strawberry.

John Wesley preached his fiery message of Methodism from the pulpit of St Michael's in 1733, whilst staying at nearby Buckland Rectory (see walk 21).

- Turn right to walk between the church and the wall, to reach a wall-enclosed footpath in the far corner of the churchyard.

- Follow the enclosed footpath to a stile leading into a field.

- Maintain your line of advance across the field, passing beneath telegraph wires to reach a stile beside a gate.

- Cross the stile and keep straight on along a clear grassy path, ignoring side turns and following the path around the hillside to a stile beside a gate.

- Cross the stile and go half-right up the next field.

- Pass through a line of trees and keep ahead, around the hillside, woods on your right hand.

- When the trees on your right end, keep straight on to a stile that comes into view in the hedge ahead.

- Cross the stile and footbridge and go half-left across the field to a stile beside a gate.

- Cross the stile and maintain your line of advance across the next field, to a gate on the skyline ahead.

- Go through the gate and maintain the same line of advance, passing a waymark post in the middle of a line of trees and then keeping ahead to a gate.

- Go through the kissing gate and keep ahead through a band of trees.

- At a track on the far side of the trees, turn right to a gate in the top corner of the field.

- Go through the gate and keep ahead up a sunken track, climbing steadily.

- Go through another gate and keep ahead up the track, which soon levels out as it contours around the slope.

Broadway Tower is visible to your right, a landmark dominating the Cotswolds skyline in this area. The tower has no historic significance: it was built in 1800 by the Earl of Coventry as a gothic folly to enhance the view from his nearby home of Croome Court.

Snowshill village.

- Pass through a wooden gate and turn right into an enclosed cross track (the Cotswolds Way).

- At another T-junction, ignore a turn to the right but keep ahead along the waymarked, enclosed track.

- Where a drive from a farm joins from the left, keep straight on along the track, following the crest of the Cotswolds.

- At a junction of tracks, DO NOT turn right with the Cotswolds Way but instead keep straight on.

- The track soon becomes a surfaced lane. Ignore a waymarked turn to the right but keep ahead along the lane.

- In 250 yards, just before a ruined cottage on the right, turn left over a stile, at a National Trust sign. Follow the track into Littleworth Wood.

- Follow the track down through the woods, ignoring side turns, to reach a stile into a field.

- Cross the stile and go half-left down the field, aiming for a gate in line with a house seen ahead.

- Go through the gate into a lane and turn right.

- At a T-junction in 150 yards, turn left.

- Follow the lane to a second T-junction in another 200 yards. Here turn left again and follow the road downhill back into the village of Snowshill.

- Follow the road back through the village to the car park.